Embracing the Transformation

Riding the Energies of the Shift with Ease and Passion

First Edition Design Publishing

ASCENSION – Embracing the Transformation
Copyright ©2015 Vidya Frazier

ISBN 978-1506-900-60-5 PRINT
ISBN 978-1506-900-61-2 EBOOK

LCCN 201556274

November 2015

Published and Distributed by
First Edition Design Publishing, Inc.
P.O. Box 20217, Sarasota, FL 34276-3217
www.firsteditiondesignpublishing.com

ASCENSION

Embracing the Transformation

Riding the Energies of the Shift
with Ease and Passion

Vidya Frazier

Table of Contents

Preface..i

Introduction 1

Chapter 1 Ascending to the Fifth Dimension 3
    A New World 4
    What is Ascension? 6
    The Fifth Dimension 6
    Returning Home 7
    The Inner Shift... 8
    Flow of this Book 11
    We're All in This Together 11

Chapter 2 Awakening, Enlightenment & Ascension Are They All the Same? 13
    Awakening...13
    Enlightenment..14
    Ascension 18
    Looking Past the Terms 19

Releasing Third-Dimensional Consciousness..21

Chapter 3 Experiencing Ascension Clean-Out..23
    One Challenge after Another 24
    Understanding the Clean-Out Process 24
    Awareness of the Larger Context..25
    Experiencing the Void 26
    Voids are Unavoidable..29
    Financial-Survival Challenges 31
    Plateaus in the Awakening Process 32
    Fears of Awakening...33
    "Fixing" Ourselves is Not the Answer 34
    Look at What Has Changed 35
    Gratitude for the Challenges...36
    Learning the Higher Purpose 38

Chapter 4 Learning to Ride the Ascension Energies 41
    Ascension Symptoms 41
    Depression, Anxiety & Despair...42
    Mood Swings...43

Hypersensitivity..44

Loss...45

Boredom 48

Mind Attacks 50

Memory Loss..50

Disorientation 51

Picking up Energy from the Collective 52

Pushed and Shoved and Stretched 53

Three Ways to Meet the Ascension Energies.................................54

Letting the Ascension Energies Carry You 55

Psychic Attacks...55

The Waves Come and Go 60

Quick Keys for Handling Ascension Stress....................................60

Chapter 5 The Body's Ascension Process....................................65

Biological Upgrades..65

Common Physical Ascension Symptoms 66

Nervous System Recalibration 66

"Ascension Flu"...67

Exhaustion, Sleep, and More Exhaustion 68

Energetic Exhaustion 68

Time to Slow Down 69

Our Bodies are Trying to Catch Up with Us 72

Energetic Tools for Healing Our Bodies.......................................73

Shift in Attitude 75

Shift in Diet 75

Beliefs about Aging...77

A Startling Reverse-Aging Experience 78

An Indication of What's to Come? 79

Aging, Ascension, and "Youthening" 79

Creating a Higher Dimensional Perspective.................................80

Chapter 6 Shifting Relationships 83

Dissolution of Karmic Bonds...83

Looking at Our Old 3D Relationship Patterns 84

3D Dependence in Relationships..85

The Freedom in 5D Relationships..86

Shifting Primary Relationships 87

Clearing of Past Relationships 88

Shifting Relationships with our Parents 90

Shifting Relationships with Our Children.....................................95

Relating Soul-to-Soul 100

When Karma is Complete...100
Soul Families Gathering..101

Chapter 7 New Relationships with Spiritual Teachers 103
Teachers Who "Fall"..104
Awakening with a Guru 105
Teachers who Bring us to our Knees 107
Experiencing Ourselves as Love..108

Chapter 8 Learning to Love Ourselves 109
What is the "Self" We Need to Love?...109
Building Ourselves up vs..110
Tearing Ourselves Down 110
Letting Go of Self-Judgment..112
Speaking Back to the Superego 112
Taking Charge...113
Inhabiting the "Center of Your Head" 116
The Controllers 117
Unworthiness is on its Way Out 118
Shift in Self-Love 118
Discovering Love Rather than Developing It 120
Making Decisions Based in Self-Love...120

Chapter 9 Letting Go of 3D Habit Patterns 123
Operating in the Fourth Dimension 123
Shifting From 3D Habit Patterns 124
Believing We're the Body-Mind...124
Believing We Need to Worry about Survival....................................125
Believing We're Unworthy...126
Getting Caught up in the World's Suffering 126
Keeping Ourselves Small...127
Focusing on What's Wrong with Us 128
Creating New 5D Habits...129

Entering into Fifth Dimensional Consciousness........................ 131

Chapter 10 Opening to the Invisible Worlds............................. 133
Accessing Inner Guidance...133
Avoiding Lower-Vibrational Entities..134
The Importance of Discernment..135
Relationship with Our Spirit Guides..135
Opening to Our Galactic Heritage...139

Working with the 144
Archangels & Ascended Masters 144
We Are All Magnificent Beings..146
Heart Opening Experience 146
We Are So Much More Than We Think We Are 147
We Are Re-Awakening 148
The Veils are Thinning..148

Chapter 11 Miracles Abounding **151**
Miracle Healing...152
Miracle Communication 154
Miracle on Mt. Shasta 157
Miracle Manifestation 158
Miracle Consciousness..163

Chapter 12 Recognizing Fifth-Dimensional Consciousness...........**165**
Common Aspects of Fifth-Dimensional Consciousness 166
Trust in the Benevolence of the Universe................................166
Openness to the "Impossible" Happening 167
Heart Expansion..167
Living in the Present Moment 168
Joy, Peace, Contentment 168
Full-On Experiences of 5D Consciousness..............................169
Floating in the Sea of Love 170
Tsunami of Love 171
How to Get There..172

Chapter 13 The Disappearing Self **175**
"Not All Here" 176
The Absent Self...177
The Observer Self...178
The Emerging Fifth-Dimensional Self 178
The Disappearing Third/Fourth-Dimensional Self 179
Living with the Disappearing Self...180

Chapter 14 Choosing To Be an Ascension Light Worker **181**
Not All Lightworkers are Ascension Lightworkers....................181
Completion of the Bodhisattva Vow......................................182
Specific Preparations for Ascension Lightworkers....................183
Valuing our Current Friends 184

Chapter 15 Shifting Identity **187**

Are the Shifts Permanent? 187

Shift in Mood 188

Shift in Self-Confidence...190

Disappearing Monkey Mind 192

Energetic Shift in Sense of Self...193

A Larger Self...193

A Higher Perspective 194

Merging with the Soul 195

Thinking from the Heart 196

Developing Psychic Abilities 196

Shifts in Everyday Life 198

Increased Synchronicities and Manifestation 199

Speeding up Our Ascension Process...199

Soul Missions 200

Chapter 16 Ascension Is Happening **203**

There's No Avoiding Ascension 203

The Game Is Over...204

Choosing To Be Wayshowers, Guides and Scouts....................204

Appendix What Are Dimensions? **207**

Resources.. **214**

Acknowledgments **215**

Preface

There are some of us who know beyond a doubt we have incarnated in this lifetime with a particular purpose: to assist humanity and the Earth in our own unique ways through the process of rapid spiritual awakening that is now occurring across the planet.

This awakening is an evolutionary leap that has been predicted throughout the ages by visionaries, indigenous elders, and a number of spiritual teachers world-wide. Referred to as *the Shift* or *Ascension to the Fifth Dimension*, it involves a radical shift from the prevailing consciousness of humanity for many thousands of years to one that is dramatically more aware, loving, interconnected and free.

For just about all of us who know we are here to be involved in assisting with this Shift, as soon as we began hearing or reading about it, something deep within us responded. Something woke up, giving birth to a deep longing to move as quickly as possible into the work we knew we were here to do.

Among other names, we've been called "Ascension Lightworkers", the "First Wave of Ascension", or "Conscious Evolutionaries". We know we are not simply here to be of service to people in traditional ways. Nor are we only waking up for our own personal spiritual evolution. We are here for the collective.

Many others, although not especially called to serve in this specific way, are also sensing that something dramatically different is happening on the planet and in their own lives. In particular, they are experiencing an acceleration in their awakening process.

My first book on this subject, *Awakening to the Fifth Dimension: A Guide for Navigating the Global Shift,* was an attempt to reach those having these kinds of experiences, offering the larger picture of the phenomenon of Ascension to explain them. I especially hoped to connect with those who might be feeling alone and confused about the changes they were experiencing and wondering what to do with their longing to move into their spiritual or life purpose. It has been heart-warming to find that the book has found and assisted many of those people.

With this book, I am hoping to give an update on the inner changes that a number of us have been experiencing since I wrote the first book in early 2014. I think I speak for many of us when I say that our Ascension experience thus far has been two-fold: We've experienced some incredibly exciting shifts, healings and openings; and we've also found that flowing with the profound changes taking place within us has proved to be a more complex mission than we once imagined. The challenging aspects of the process have perhaps also gone on longer than we'd imagined.

Most of us within this Ascension Lightworker group are deeply familiar with life's challenging invitations; we've gone through many years of working through our "stuff", developing solid spiritual practices, and healing our bodies. We've survived difficult relationships, profound losses, and dramatic inner and outer changes in our lives.

And I believe a lot of us assumed or hoped, in our initial optimism about the Shift, that it would simply require a little more of what we'd already experienced. The one difference might be that, with the excitement of what the big picture was all about, we could move through all that was necessary with relative ease and joy. For many, this has not proven to be so.

Through the counseling and healing work I offer and through listening to others I know, I have kept track of many people who know they are here to assist with the Shift. I can see that with certain people, some discouragement is settling in as they realize just how endless their "third-dimensional baggage" seems to be and how difficult at times it is to release it. I myself have felt this to some degree, as time has gone on and more and more continues to surface that I am called to own, accept and let go of.

However, if I look more closely, I also see deep inner changes and awakenings many of us have been experiencing through the last few years. Although we may still be facing some intense challenges in our lives, we are freer, wiser, stronger and more awake—and not just because some time has passed. The awakening that has happened has been of a specific nature—both profound and rapid—and has shown us, at least at times, the startling beauty of who each of us is as a radiant being of light.

Thus the impetus behind this book is to report what I am witnessing in people now going through the Ascension process at this point, so that readers can see they are not alone in their experiences, and they can also identify more clearly what their own experiences are.

My purpose is also to give encouragement to those who may be struggling with uncertainty about what they've chosen to do this lifetime—encouragement to continue to move through the intense shifting, loss, and confusion they may be experiencing.

I do this through sharing much about my own Ascension journey and also that of many other people I work with and know. I write about our challenges; but I also point out and describe the many exciting shifts of consciousness I am seeing, as well.

The changes I've experienced and noted in others have been so rapid that this book has been difficult to write. Often in this process I found that what I'd written just six months before was no longer accurate. Too much had changed in that short period of time. Also several times I thought the book was finally complete, only to realize there were suddenly many more things I needed to add— experiences and phenomena that had not been happening earlier.

At some point I simply had to just call it quits and see this book as a "slice of life" within a period of time in the Ascension process. And to realize that even a few months after publishing it, some of what I'd written might no longer be relevant or perhaps even true.

At any rate, my hope is that in reading this, you will be able to relate to what I've described and that you will have insights into the depth of awakening that is likely occurring within you, whether you've been fully aware of it or not.

And with this understanding, perhaps you can continue on with renewed enthusiasm and optimism—and hopefully even passion— on this wild and mysterious journey into the Fifth Dimension you've signed up for this lifetime.

Vidya Frazier
October 2015

Introduction

Chapter 1

Ascending to the Fifth Dimension

There's no doubt the world is rapidly changing around us. Something monumental is happening, impacting our lives in increasingly intense ways. Most people are not consciously aware of this yet. They continue on, often assuming more and more stress in their lives, but without stopping to wonder what might be causing it.

However, there are many of who have noticed the dramatic shift the world and our lives have taken in the last few years and are experiencing profound and unusual experiences within ourselves. We realize we are growing and awakening much more quickly than ever before.

In looking at my own life, I can certainly say this is so for me. Indeed, there are times when I feel that the changes I've experienced are so great, I don't even know myself anymore.

I look at myself from some removed place and scratch my head, wondering: "Who *is* this person? What happened to all that self-doubt she used to carry around? Where is her tendency to hide? And—when did she get so darned *happy*?"

In three short years I feel I've become such a different person, it boggles my mind. Like many of us on a spiritual path, during the many decades of spiritual growth work I engaged in, I observed a number of positive changes in myself. I was becoming more awake, more authentic, more peaceful and free.

But it all took place very gradually, over a long period of time. What I've experienced in the last few years has been radical—both in the nature of the change I've experienced and in the speed at which it has taken place.

Perhaps most surprising is that I have been experiencing for the first time in my life an ongoing sense of what I simply call "human happiness". After feeling a default sense of depression constantly tugging on me all my life, I am now generally living in an unfamiliar field of happiness, quite often for no reason at all. I also experience a sense of self-confidence and inner power I could never seem to achieve previously.

The monkey mind I used to struggle with is all but gone. I experience a merging with what I clearly perceive to be my Soul, experience a dramatic opening of psychic abilities, and know myself to be a large and powerful energetic being. Very importantly, I am finally experiencing financial abundance and am blessed to have work I find deeply gratifying. And, at long last, I have been experiencing a miraculous healing of certain body symptoms that have plagued me for years.

What has happened here? How did all this appear in such a short period of time? If I were the only one this kind of rapid change was happening to, I could just shrug and assign it all to one of the many mysteries that just seem to happen in life.

But many, many others I know and read about are reporting the same things happening in their lives. Huge shifts are taking place and new, more highly evolved versions of themselves are being born in dramatically rapid ways.

This hasn't happened for any of us with great ease. There have been countless bumps in the road—periods of painful loss, deep emotional release, and constant vigilance to not fall prey to old patterns of negativity. At times the quest for a sense of balance and inner peace has been intense and exhausting. In addition, there's been an inner demand that we continually move forward through unfamiliar terrain of consciousness.

Yet through it all we have been aware that there has always been an inner beacon of light—however flickering at times—showing us the way into the birthing of a new, higher-vibrational self.

For many of us experiencing this phenomenal change, it's not really a surprise that it's occurring. We understand that we are simply experiencing our personal version of a global phenomenon of rapid transformation that seems to be occurring across the world ever since December 2012.

A New World

Indeed, at one point the solstice of December 21, 2012 was a magical date for many people eagerly awaiting what they thought would be the end of our current world—and the beginning of a new and glorious one in which peace, harmony and oneness would reign.

Misunderstanding the Mayan prophecies and other predictions made by visionaries and spiritual teachers about the ending of an eons-long cycle in human history, they believed we'd be finishing the cycle overnight. And that we'd wake up the following morning to a whole new world in which we'd all be, at the very least, enlightened.

This misinterpretation was understandable. There was certainly a lot of hype out there and excited proclamations being made by channels and spiritual teachers about that date that would lead people to think this way.

But as I explained in my first book on this subject, *Awakening to the Fifth Dimension: A Guide for Navigating the Global Shift,* what actually happened in December 2012 is that we did indeed complete a very long evolutionary cycle on that date (indeed a number of cycles); however, we did not suddenly enter into a new awakened world overnight. Instead, we entered onto a "bridge" between the two worlds which we will be living on for a while as the new world gradually emerges.

If viewed on an evolutionary scale, the short amount of time it will probably take for this new awakened world to emerge— probably within the lifetime of many of us now alive—is truly miraculous. However, it will take much more time yet for the transformation to be complete.

There will be much happening while on this bridge, some of it as difficult as it will be liberating. But it has been foretold in many prophecies world-wide that at some point in the not too distant future we will be entering fully into a Golden Age of awakened humanity on the Earth.

According to many esoteric teachings, Golden Ages have happened previously in the history of the Earth. About every 26,000 years the Earth enters the center of the Milky Way, as it is currently doing. In this area of the galaxy, high frequencies of energy exist that naturally lift all planets and beings that move through this field into a higher vibration of consciousness, greatly accelerating the rate of evolution.

There are two basic paradigms that describe this rapid evolutionary shift humanity and the Earth are currently experiencing. One is known simply as the *Shift* and is described by certain visionaries and spiritual teachers today who sometimes identify themselves as *conscious evolutionaries*. The other is known as *Ascension*.

Although I use both terms interchangeably throughout this book, the Ascension paradigm speaks more clearly to me, as it describes in greater detail all aspects of what is occurring during this transition. For those who are new to the Ascension paradigm and its terminology, let me briefly describe more of the process to which it refers.

What is Ascension?

Ascension describes the particular process of rapid spiritual awakening that is happening to varying degrees to ever-increasing numbers of people across the planet at this time, along with the inevitable societal change that accompanies this. We can see this awakening unfolding outwardly in a variety of ways in the world, most noticeably in the political, social and economic arenas. And many of us are also experiencing it as a force moving through us personally.

In describing this awakening in the context of Ascension, humanity is seen to be shifting from one dimension or level of consciousness to another more evolved one. The state of consciousness we've recently left is called the *Third Dimension*. The bridge we're now on is understood to be the *Fourth Dimension*. And where we're headed is the *Fifth Dimension*.

The Fifth Dimension

The Fifth Dimension is the level of consciousness many of us have been dreaming about and praying for, probably for many lifetimes. It's where we will finally awaken into full consciousness of who we are and live in the absolute knowing of the oneness of all that exists. It is where we will be able to live from a state of unconditional love, inner peace and joy, and on-going freedom from fear, shame, judgment and separation.

According to the teachings on Ascension, we are all heir to fifth-dimensional consciousness. It's a state of being we once lived in many thousands of years ago, before the advent of what's known as the "Fall of Consciousness", a time when we began descending into the lower vibrational field that's the Third Dimension.

This lower dimension was a level of being in the universe that allowed for a new expression for Consciousness to manifest itself through: life in a dense, physical form. But it also brought with it many confining limitations, a forgetting of our divine nature, a sense of separation from each other and from the Divine, and experiences of great suffering.

Many of us have been incarnating over and over again into the Earth's Third Dimension for the thousands of years since the Fall of Consciousness. So it is near-impossible for us to remember the experience of living in the Fifth Dimension. What we remember is the suffering present in the Third Dimension and the challenges in remembering who we actually are—powerful, multi-dimensional beings of Light living in full consciousness of our essential spiritual nature.

(For a fuller description of the Fifth Dimension, and also of the Third and Fourth Dimensions, please see the Appendix entitled "What are Dimensions?".)

Returning Home

Those unending experiences of suffering and limitation in the Third Dimension are now over. Although there will be a final playing out of many of the third-dimensional energies on the world scene for a while to come, the door to that dimension has shut behind us.

We have now entered a time of rapid evolution when the whole "adventure" (or "experiment") of dwelling in the Third Dimension is coming to an end. With this completion we are now crossing the fourth-dimensional bridge, finally returning at long last to a Home in the Fifth Dimension.

Although I initially resisted this paradigm of Ascension as being simplistic and totally unrealistic when I first encountered it, I eventually began seeing that it made sense of everything I could see happening in the world at this time, both in the collective and within myself and other individuals I knew.

Over time I began receiving more and more inner teachings about what was happening during this transition. I also began having memories of the distant past and experiencing dramatic shifts of consciousness—and I realized I was resonating more and more with the Ascension teachings I was reading and hearing about. I now hold a deep knowing within me of the truth they hold.

It's true that much still looks and feels chaotic in the world at this time—in fact, not much different from what life on Earth has looked like as far back as anyone can remember. Violence, war, hatred, and domination still reign in many places around the globe.

Indeed, unrest and violence are erupting more forcefully than ever in certain locations. In addition, the global economy is increasingly unstable, and climate change presents unthinkable possibilities for the future. It's natural to conclude that things are definitely getting worse and even that humanity may be on its way to extinction.

However, if we observe closely, we can see that there is much happening, often unreported by mainstream media, that is definitely optimistic and reflective of a world that is beginning to heal itself. There is much available, especially if we follow the alternative and international news on the internet, which describes the myriad ways in which the Shift is currently manifesting in the world.

Across the globe people are waking up from thousands of years of suppression and control and for the first time no longer passively accepting these inherited circumstances. Wide-spread corruption is being revealed in age-old political, financial, social, and religious structures that have traditionally ruled us through exploitation, greed, control and enslavement. And we see them now crumbling and falling down around us.

At the same time fresh new energies are abounding at the grass roots level to create new societal structures based on values of cooperation, harmony, kindness, justice and equality. Many in the younger generations are stepping forward without the constraints or limitations older generations have had and are creating breakthrough possibilities for helping people to live in new and freer ways. These descriptions and accounts are incredibly uplifting and inspiring.

The Inner Shift

Although all of this occurring in the world is extremely exciting to me—indeed, signs of it often bring tears of deep joy—my own particular interest has always been on the inner personal experience of the Shift: the Ascension process that I believe is happening in one way or another inside all of us who have chosen, either consciously or unconsciously, to ascend to the Fifth Dimension of consciousness.

People sometimes ask if everybody is going to be making this shift into higher consciousness; they can't imagine this happening when they look at the world as it is now. The teachings tell us that there are a number of people who, on the soul level, have not chosen to do this at this time. They will be leaving the planet before the Earth makes its final shift. As Souls, they will be taken to other places in the universe where the Third Dimension is still in existence for further evolutionary progress.

But for those of us who have chosen to make the transition at this point, I am seeing that something new and precious is being born within us and can be known if we stop and begin to notice it. In my experience, it's showing up in various ways within all of us. For some, it's very subtle and as yet not quite recognizable. For others, it's very apparent.

It might be described as a fresh new awareness that is awakening within us—a new sense of ease and grace in our lives: a deeper understanding about life and ourselves, an ability to live more consistently from a place of love and understanding, and a profound sense of peace we've never known before.

Many of us currently on a conscious path of Ascension have been awakening spiritually for a number of years. Indeed, a good number of us began our journeys back in the 60s and 70s during those times of great social, political and spiritual awakening. We each found our unique paths toward inner freedom and have been diligently following them toward greater awakening, step by step.

But many within this group, I am finding, are now feeling that something is shifting but not knowing what it is. The spiritual practices they've always used are somehow no longer serving them as they once did. There's a sense of energetic intensity they're encountering—and yet also a flatness or lack of direction, a question of "So now what?" Without understanding about the Shift that's occurring, it can be confusing and unsettling.

In some ways, the Ascension process is no different from the long and gradual awakening process many of us have been involved in over the last decades. But it's clear that awakening has gradually been accelerating over the last five to ten years.

And in the last few years since 2012—and even in the last few months—the process has started to take off with a speed that can be breath-taking. As I've mentioned, certain profound changes I've observed in myself have been startling and unexpected, and I see similar kinds of changes occurring in many others that I work with, as well.

This process is exhilarating. And yet it also brings with it many challenges—as, in the process, we are compelled to let go of age-old beliefs and ways of operating, sometimes in very rapid and abrupt ways.

At times, old dysfunctional patterns we've managed to somehow live with for years are now in our faces, demanding to be given up. For some of us, loss is showing up in our relationships, our work, our finances, our very sense of identity. We are being called to enter into the Unknown and live solely by trust and intuition.

All of this can bring up fear and anxiety, at times wreaking havoc in our relationships, our work and our health. We watch as our egos play out their last efforts in maintaining control, trying to create safety and fulfillment in all the unsuccessful ways they've always used.

And yet this Ascension process can also bring us great joy, as well—as we see how, in being willing to drop what is no longer working, we witness great transformation taking place within us. Sometimes this is in subtle ways, and at other times it's with great clarity. And as this happens, we watch as the deeper, more alive and expansive Self we've always been emerges from beneath the layers of old third-dimensional disguise.

I have no doubt about this dynamic of Ascension operating in my own life. It truly feels like a process of ascending into a higher, lighter, freer sense of being—spacious and yet very grounded at the same time. And I know on a deep intuitive level it is happening, or is beginning to happen, to every one of us on the planet who has signed up for it this time around.

As we are all unique beings taking this journey, it's playing out differently within each of our lives. But I believe there are common themes we're all experiencing. I will be describing and reflecting on these themes throughout this book. I will also bring up questions that are arising in many of us as we travel ever more deeply into the unknown territory of the Fourth and Fifth Dimensions and learn to embrace the transformation we see taking place.

Flow of this Book

The next chapter of this book presents a further discussion of what Ascension is about on the conceptual level as an introduction for those not familiar with this paradigm.

Following that is a section entitled "Releasing Third-Dimensional Consciousness", an exploration of what appears to be a "clean-out" aspect of the Ascension process. Most of what I describe here are the more challenging aspects of the Ascension process I am witnessing.

The last section, called "Entering into Fifth Dimensional Consciousness", features descriptions of new openings and experiences people describe having. These chapters reveal the exciting and expansive nature of experiences that tend to over-ride and balance the challenging aspects of the clean-out experiences.

We're All in This Together

It brings me indescribable joy when I tune into this rapid awakening occurring within each one of us on the planet who have chosen to make the transition. In my inner vision I clearly see us on a long and wide path—all walking along together toward Home after a long, long time spent in a foreign land.

We're each on various parts of this path—some further ahead, some behind—but we're all here moving in groups of familiar Souls around us. In our higher consciousness, we're celebrating with incredible relief and joy that we are finally leaving our time in the Third Dimension behind and are returning Home to full consciousness once again.

This image is deep and very real inside me. It's clear to me that as humanity, we truly are one divine Being, one collective consciousness—with an infinite variety of individual expressions. The mystery of how we can be just one consciousness—and yet many unique sparks of consciousness, simultaneously—confounds the rational mind. And yet I believe this mystery is known and experienced without paradox or confusion deep within each one of us.

With profound love for all my sisters and brothers traveling with me on this path Home, I offer my reflections on this radiantly wondrous journey of Ascension in which we're all engaged. My hope is that these reflections will help inspire reflections on your own journey and that they will give you support and insight as you travel on your chosen path Home.

I invite you here to walk with me. Let us go hand in hand together with passion in our hearts, laughing when we can, supporting each other through the rough spots, and singing the song of joy that has been playing in our Souls since we first sprang forth into being from the Godhead, eons ago.

Chapter 2

Awakening, Enlightenment & Ascension
Are They All the Same?

It may be helpful for me to first of all attempt to define and describe the term *Ascension* a bit more in the way I use it. I find we often use words like this with others, thinking we're talking about the same thing; but we actually have something very different in mind, based on our unique understandings and personal experiences. And it can get confusing if we don't at least attempt to define what we're talking about.

One way I can describe what I mean by *Ascension* is to clarify what relationship, if any, the term has to certain other similar-sounding concepts in my vocabulary such as *awakening* and *enlightenment*.

Awakening

I find the term *awakening* to be an especially broad term that is used by people to mean a number of very different things. Some use it to describe social, political or psychological awareness; others to indicate what they happen to understand spiritual awakening to be; and still others to indicate an awareness of unusual phenomena existing beyond the understanding of the rational mind, such as extra terrestrial beings and UFOs.

For me, *awakening* can refer to all these states of consciousness. There are many levels of awakening and also many different realms of reality into which we can awaken. But generally, I've personally used the term since my very first experiences in opening to realms of consciousness beyond the five senses. When I first became aware that my inner experiences had a context called *awakening*, I found it a very useful word.

In the early days on my spiritual path during the '60s and '70s, I was mostly involved with teachings of Western metaphysics and

h, and all this was generally thrown together by
round me and called "awakening", "spiritual
spiritual growth."

these concepts to refer to a slow and gradual path
of opening up to the mysteries that lay beyond the understanding
of the rational mind. It was a process of learning about spiritual
realities, working off karma, shedding the ego, and waking up to my
higher, "spiritual self".

There was the reference point of eventually getting off the
wheel of karma—that all of us awakening were on a path with the
goal of finally becoming free of karma and not having to come back
to Earth to continue on with countless lives of suffering. The
concept of "God" was part of this paradigm; there was God and
there were Souls striving to "get back to" and "be one with" God.

I had read a smattering of books during those early years
coming from the Eastern traditions and knew of the concept of
enlightenment but didn't totally relate to it at the time, so I didn't
use it a lot. And the concept of Ascension hadn't really come on the
scene yet, so I didn't feel any confusion about these terms at that
time.

Later, as I'll explain below, I did encounter the terms and
experiences of both enlightenment and Ascension, and then some
confusion came into the picture.

Enlightenment

I actually hesitate these days to use the word *enlightenment* at
all, due to the fact that people seem to have so many different
interpretations of what it is. It's not surprising when, first of all,
Eastern texts translated into English describe many different kinds
of enlightenment that exist, such as *fourth-chakra enlightenment*,
cosmic consciousness, God-Realization, Sahaja Samadhi, and *Moksha*,
to just name a few.

But then, when Westerners began taking over the use of the
term *enlightenment* in the last forty years or so, it became even
more complicated, as many started incorporating the Western
concepts of "personal growth" and "spiritual growth" into it.

It has become even further complicated in the last couple of
decades since Western teachers giving satsangs (spiritual
teachings) came to realize that many Westerners simply couldn't
relate to the sudden, spontaneous type of awakening described as

enlightenment by Eastern masters and texts and were getting upset because they weren't experiencing it. Most people in satsangs were, instead, having a gradual experience of waking up to the kind of freedom the Eastern texts spoke of.

Some of these teachers also recognized that there were certain people in their groups who did understand this experience because they'd actually had an "enlightenment experience" that seemed to be very real—but then these students would somehow eventually "lose" the experience down the road.

And to complicate the matter even further, in the past ten years or so, I've noticed that certain Western teachers who used to speak about enlightenment as an experience of knowing oneself as that which is beyond form—simply Consciousness or Awareness, as many Eastern texts do—are not focusing on that understanding as much anymore. They're realizing that what is needed more and more is the experience of an "embodied" enlightenment, an enlightenment that ordinary people carry with them into their everyday lives.

We're living in very different times from those referred to in Eastern spiritual texts written centuries ago. These days, we don't generally have the luxury of moving into a monastery when enlightenment has happened in order to be with an enlightened master and have the experience nurtured and firmly established. We have to get up the next day and get the kids off to school and spend our day at work.

With all this in mind, in order to further clarify what my own reference point of the term enlightenment is as I speak about it, I will briefly share an experience I've had (and that I described in my first book the Art of Letting Go) that I would classify as enlightenment in the more traditional sense.

One evening a number of years ago, out of nowhere, I experienced a sudden and spontaneous shift into an entirely different knowing of myself—a realization that I was pure Awareness. All sense of being an individual body-mind had evaporated. There was no longer a "me".

An indescribable spaciousness and bliss enveloped me for many months with this transformation, as I now knew myself absolutely to be one with all of existence. I floated through life with a natural joy and buoyancy and there was a complete loss of any sense of suffering.

All striving or seeking for anything was gone; what was present was a simple and effortless acceptance of whatever was arising—along with a profound love for all that existed and a deep gratitude for life in all its manifest forms.

I think I speak for many of us who have had these kinds of experiences that, after a time, the on-going full and total experience of myself as simply clear and empty Consciousness, beyond any individual form—and the transcendent bliss that accompanied this—eventually began dissipating. And about six months after the experience, the sense of being an individual entity eventually reappeared.

This happened slowly at first; but eventually, within four or five years, I was once again experiencing myself most often as an individual consciousness with a personality. Much to my chagrin, this again became my "default" consciousness. And although I can still within a moment's notice move into the experience of knowing myself simply as empty Awareness (and feel the bliss of this), I do have to focus on it first before I experience it.

Yet what has never dissipated is the profound understanding of my true nature that was revealed and experienced. And much of that original realization has remained with me and is lived through me today. It might take a moment when something challenging happens, but very quickly I can usually access a peaceful, relaxed acceptance of whatever is occurring, knowing that I am simply the field of Consciousness in which everything is happening.

Transcendent Enlightenment

I now identify that experience as a *transcendent enlightenment* experience. I fully realized myself as that which exists beyond and before form. There is an exquisite sense of freedom known in this experience that I believe cannot be experienced if there is still any kind of identification with something singular and individual. And there is a profound peace that comes with such a realization that is beyond any I've experienced since the sense of individuality has returned to me.

I was fortunate enough to be able to go to India back in the early 1990s to see the spiritual master Papaji, who gave me validation for what had occurred for me. Being with him anchored my realization for the following years and has probably helped me to retain as much of the experience as I have today.

I think there may be many people who have an enlightenment awakening like this who do not get that kind of validation and therefore have no reference point for it, and it unfortunately dissipates or disappears without their full understanding of what has occurred.

Embodied Enlightenment

What eventually became apparent to me in the years following this awakening was that there was still something missing. Even if I had retained the full experience of it, I believe I would have still known something was missing.

It was true that, even after the experience eventually dissipated, I continued to feel profoundly peaceful and very accepting of whatever flowed into my life. Life was simply happening. I experienced a sense of liberating detachment from most things and people I'd been attached to before. And I lived with a deep sense of freedom, knowing I could always within a moment shift into the experience of who I was beyond the form and personality.

And yet I eventually realized that what was missing was a sense of true joy about life—a happiness about being alive here in this body. I lacked the experience of totally embodying my awakening. I was still reaching out to the Nothingness that I was in order to feel the freedom and the peace that nurtured me. Something in me knew that as powerful as the enlightenment experience had been, it had been an incomplete awakening: I needed to somehow bring it down more fully into my body and into my everyday life.

Although I hadn't done as complete a job at what's been called a "spiritual bypass" as some people I knew, I had in my own way tried to do it. I had tried to leap-frog over all my still-unresolved personality issues. Many of them had been burned away by my experience; but others still remained.

I was still bumping up against certain psychological issues I'd never fully resolved in both my relationships and my work. I knew that in a certain way, I had to "back up" on my path. I had to recognize that I had "plateaued out" and that I wouldn't get any further until I dealt with these issues.

And with that realization, I had to eat some rather distasteful humble pie. After initial resistance, I once again became involved with teachings that taught about gradual awakening and that helped me to focus on myself as a Soul having a relationship with God (rather than simply knowing myself *as* God).

In the enlightenment experience, it was clear there was no separation between God and me—indeed, the concept of God was actually irrelevant. It was evident that form itself—including any sense of an individual self—was illusion. And yet I realized that this new path I was beginning to take was necessary if I were to truly return to full consciousness. A certain amount of healing was still necessary; I needed to experience a fully embodied enlightenment.

Ascension

It was at this point that I began looking at the Ascension teachings that were out there and feeling a surprising resonance to them. And I began trying to decipher what the experience of Ascension and being in the Fifth Dimension were really about. Was this the same experience as enlightenment—simply a Western esoteric way of describing it?

If I looked at the transcendent enlightenment experience I'd had, it sure didn't sound like it. Ascension teachings I was aware of spoke of our discovering that we are each a magnificent Being of light. They pointed to the individual uniqueness of each Soul. In the Fifth Dimension, we would each be operating and creating from our uniqueness as Souls. It would be our first step back to the "Creator", Source or God. I realized that perhaps Ascension to the Fifth Dimension was more like what I'd come to see "embodied enlightenment" to mean.

And yet, eventually, I began hearing references, both inwardly and outwardly, of what happens in the Sixth Dimension and higher—and a bell would go off in me. I'd hear how form becomes more and more elusive in the higher realms and the experience of knowing ourselves is no longer as separate individuals; rather we become part of a collective consciousness or "unity consciousness".

This sounded closer to what my transcendent enlightenment experience had been—especially since, as we travel further into the higher dimensions, we apparently become more and more simply Consciousness, with no reference point of individuality at all. And recently I have begun having experiences of being part of what does feel like a collective consciousness, and these feel similar to those experiences of knowing myself as pure Consciousness.

But a while back, before I began having these experiences of the dimensions higher than the Fifth Dimension, I was brought to the question of "Why not just skip to that level of knowing myself as

Consciousness again—and forget about all this waking up to myself as a multidimensional individual being? Why not just keep going for the gold?"

Yet when I'd ask this, I realized that a deep part of me was answering, "But I *want* to play this game! I want to experience myself as a beautiful, free, creative human being in a light body. I want to experience full human happiness and clear unconditional love for myself and everyone else while in a physical body."

I realized that this was the reason I was incarnated here in form—to do this. And I saw that I was very moved by what was happening out in the world, with the Earth, and with all of humanity. I knew I was here to be part of this whole play of consciousness now unfolding within the realm of form. I wanted to experience the exciting phenomenon of Ascension.

And so I signed on. I fully and consciously decided to jump in and play with all I'm worth and all I have to give to this process of Ascension—to this particular, fascinating form of awakening. And to experience it fully, with enthusiasm, curiosity and complete commitment. I have never regretted this decision. I find it the most exciting game around—the only one, in fact, that I'm at all interested in at this point. I no longer see it as a somewhat "inferior" type of awakening, when compared to the transcendent type of awakening.

One thing I love about the experience of Ascension is the focus on the opening of the Heart and living from this space within us. Other spiritual teachings, of course, also teach this. But there is a particular focus on the Heart in the Ascension teachings—and it occurs also in my own experiences in which there is an indescribable energy with it that I don't find in other teachings. And there's the knowing that the opening of the Heart is beginning to happen to everyone on the planet at this time.

Most people who have decided as Souls to ascend are just at the beginning of this process—but it seems that many are already feeling the promptings of the Heart toward kindness, justice, compassion and peace; and this so fills me with love and hope and optimism for the human race, I want to weep with joy.

Looking Past the Terms

So, am I any closer to knowing the differences, if any, between the experiences of awakening, enlightenment and Ascension? Not really. It all continues to remain a mystery. But in laying it all out like this, it puts the issue to rest for me. My mind relaxes. I realize it really doesn't matter in the end. It's just story, stuff the mind likes to play with.

And, in very simple terms, I can simply accept that the path of awakening for those of us currently in human form involves both kinds of awakening I've described: the full realization of ourselves as pure Divine Consciousness—AND as unique individual expressions of that Consciousness.

Perhaps if you've had any wonderings, confusion, or attempts to organize your own thoughts around these concepts, you too can now lay those down and instead simply focus on what is currently occurring for you during these times without any need to define it with particular concepts or contexts.

And for now in the rest of this book, I'll just speak about "Ascension symptoms" or "signs of awakening" or whatever—and hopefully you can look past any words I use to the experiences themselves that you may recognize or have intentions for in yourself.

Releasing Third-Dimensional Consciousness

Chapter 3

Experiencing Ascension Clean-Out

So now, with more clarity about what Ascension is about conceptually, let us turn to the actual experience of it. I will share what I have noticed to be happening both within myself and many others I know and work with since the Ascension process began happening.

Some of the experiences and changes I will describe have been happening in the last ten years or so when Ascension experiences first started becoming noticeable for some of us. But I will focus mainly on the period of time since December 2012, as this most recent period has seemed to usher in the most profound changes in many of our lives.

This section of the book, entitled "Releasing Third-Dimensional Consciousness", includes information and experiences that relate to the somewhat more difficult phases that are occurring for people going through this process.

It's good to keep in mind that the challenging experiences I describe definitely come and go in our day to day lives. Often there are beautiful and uplifting experiences, such as the ones I describe in the section following this one, that are intertwined with these more difficult events.

It's not surprising that challenging experiences are arising; the shift from the Third Dimension to the Fifth Dimension is an enormous one. We are in the midst of experiencing a death process—the death of our old 3D self and all its familiar beliefs, emotions and experiences. And we are also in the midst of an enormous birth process into a brand new self that is as yet unknown to us. Both birth and death processes are generally known to be chaotic and messy at times.

It can therefore be helpful to name the specific challenges involved in this dual experience and understand why they are occurring, as we are then able to move through them with greater ease—and hopefully, even with gratitude.

One Challenge after Another

In reflecting on my own experience and observing others I know, I see that we are all going through periods of what I can only call "clean-out". Sometimes these periods last weeks, months— maybe even years for some—in which we meet one challenge after another and need to constantly focus on releasing old patterns, beliefs and emotions.

In a way, these periods of clean-out are no different from what any of us has experienced in the past; there have always been times in life when we've gone through difficult passages. And if we're fortunate, we've learned deep lessons from them and come out the other end wiser—although, at times, also more vulnerable and wounded.

But these times of clearing during the last few years of our lives since 2012 have been different in certain ways: they tend to be more intense and to pull up disturbing issues that have plagued us our entire lives. At times it can feel as if we're in a pressure cooker with energy continuing to build until we feel we might explode.

Also, there often isn't much time to fully gather our strength and inner resources after a period of clean-out before another wave hits us. Sometimes the releasing process can feel endless.

With this kind of intensity, there are times when we have to depend more than ever on all the inner strength we have access to, to simply make it through a day. If we're lucky, we also have outer resources—friends, family, therapists, healers—who can assist us in the process of dealing with the issues coming up. But many are handling the clean-out process pretty much alone.

Understanding the Clean-Out Process

It's important to understand that Ascension is not an overnight process. Nor does it just *happen* to us. There is no outside source or force that will effortlessly clear all the emotional baggage and misunderstandings about the nature of reality we have accumulated during the thousands of years we've likely existed in the Third Dimension.

It is true that waking up is somewhat easier to do than it once was, given the high frequency energies that are pouring into the

Earth now that we're in the Fourth Dimension. And we're also getting help, when we ask for it, from the archangels, ascended masters and galactics that wasn't as available before.

However, waking up is still something we have do for ourselves, something we have to focus on, something we have to continue to do—until we are eventually clear enough and resonating with the vibration of the Fifth Dimension. And for most of us, this is taking some time. It's a process.

If you really consider what full awakening to and living your spiritual nature entails, you have to acknowledge that a whole lot has to change. Not only do we need to clear out low-vibration emotions and limited beliefs from this lifetime—but also, for most of us, from many past lives as well. On top of that, our dense physical bodies need to be completely rewired. All of this is huge. And it all can't be accomplished too quickly, or we'd combust.

Awareness of the Larger Context

What's fortunate, however, is we can have a great deal more awareness now in meeting these waves of clean-out, more understanding of what they're about. We can be aware that our old unresolved issues are arising at this time so we may finally release them and move ever more securely into fifth-dimensional consciousness.

This understanding can make these periods of purging somewhat easier to endure. There's a purpose to them, an almost tangible goal—one that is more palatable and true than those we've often worked with in the past, such as having to pay back karma or feeling we are somehow broken and have to be fixed.

I have personally endured very painful clean-out experiences in my past, including years of physical illness and inability to bring in sufficient income. These past three to four years have been no different in certain ways. However, in other ways, they have been very different. I find I can now be aware of a very clear "plan" my Higher Self has for me during this time and the need to clear out old issues that have weighed me down in some cases for lifetimes.

I've also been aware of an urgency I've never felt before to move through the times of releasing. There's a subtle sense of a push inside me, a constant (though gentle) nudging to keep moving ever forward through the difficult times.

There is also a constant urging for me to stay awake to what is happening and to learn everything that is being presented to me all along the way. I have developed an on-going awakeness to the inner workings of my psyche—being as watchful as possible of my thoughts and emotions and my responses to outside stimuli.

Experiencing the Void

At one point during these past years, I enrolled in an intense program of healing and clearing through a process known as Quantum Healing, offered by healer Dell Morris; and I progressed forward with it for about three years.

During most of this time I went through what I refer to as the *Void*—a time when I felt stripped of all my old comfortable ways of experiencing life. This passage has traditionally been called a "dark night of the soul", and I've also recently heard it referred to as "Ascension Purgatory"—a very apt name.

In my own experience, at one point I began realizing that all my ego identities—all the ways in which I had always presented myself to the outer world—had fallen away. This included all the roles I had played in my career as a transpersonal psychotherapist, workshop leader, and author. It also included the familiar role of elder or mentor I'd played more recently in communities in which I'd lived.

My life became flat and boring, very small. I found I craved anonymity; for the most part, I just wanted to stay home alone. I had no interest in meeting new people or even spending time with many of my usual friends. All my past interests and passions seemed to vanish. I felt zero creativity. My life as I'd known it was finished—and I had no idea where I was going or how I would live out the rest of it. My future appeared both blank and bleak.

One thing was clear during this period, however—and that was that I was clearing out a whole lot of karmic patterns I'd brought into this lifetime. I was experiencing a total stripping down of my egoic self. There was a time when a vision of myself came to me: that of a young girl, totally naked and vulnerable, sitting on the floor alone. Around me lay broken and crumbled walls—walls that had once protected me my entire life. I was at last visible in all my nakedness to the world around me.

I initially experienced terror in this experience; but once I finally surrendered to it, I realized I was feeling an enormous sense of relief. I could finally stop trying to defend myself, present myself differently from who I really was, or create images of who I thought I wanted to be.

I was just who I was with all the flaws and weaknesses I'd always known I had. And, eventually, as I began relaxing into this new experience and realizing there was nothing I could do to change any of it, anyway, I felt a powerful sense of freedom and joy.

But it was a process. At times I was faced with tremendous challenges. There was one two-month period in which I had to find my way through a deep and dark fog of self-hatred. It seemed so powerful and ancient, as memories of who I'd been and what I'd done in past lifetimes swirled around me, that I feared I'd never find my way out of it.

Another time, I suddenly came upon a huge, ugly yellow-brown river of shame that was flowing within me—the existence of which I had always sensed semi-consciously, but had never known how to reach. This river too seemed ancient—something that had been with me for ages, lifetime after lifetime. And I had to have the courage be with that river, swimming in it to fully experience what it was, before it began to evaporate.

And yet, even through these dark experiences, I had days in which a bright and luminous feeling of joy would sustain me throughout every activity I was engaged in. Or I'd suddenly find myself filled with an unexpected peace that was so profound, it brought tears of gratitude to my eyes.

There was nothing different happening in my life when these lovely experiences would appear. They were always spontaneous, and deep awareness of who I was beyond all experience would always emerge with them. I became increasingly aware that both the pleasant and the unpleasant experiences were all of a piece—all emanating from the Ascension process. They were all part of my awakening into higher consciousness, and there was no reason to fret about any of it.

More than One Void

From what I've noticed, we usually don't simply endure just one of these Void experiences along our path of awakening. Some of us have to do it more than once, as if the process comes in stages. When I was part way through the experience I've described above, I realized I'd already gone through another one earlier in my life. That one lasted almost ten years. It happened when my marriage, my health, my work and my finances all collapsed pretty much at the same time. I was so sick and exhausted, I could barely function most days for weeks on end.

Needless to say, this was an earlier version of what was to occur later. The second experience simply served to strip my ego identification down even further. The good news was that in the second experience, I was more aware of what was happening on a deeper level, and I was therefore able to surrender more completely to my Higher Self's "tough love" embrace.

Different Flavors of Voids

Everybody's version of a Void is somewhat different. Some people experience periods of depression; others may feel rage surfacing from years of not expressing it; still others may experience free-floating anxiety.

I hear a number of people speak about a feeling of simply being "finished" with their life. It's over—and they just want to go Home. This feeling of "homesickness" can come up when there's a sense of overwhelm during a clean-out period, and a weariness descends on us. We feel we can go on no longer if things don't change pretty rapidly.

But it can also arise when we have reached a feeling of completeness and nothing else has appeared to draw our attention. There's a flatness, an emptiness we're experiencing, in which we can't imagine what else we may ever want to do with our life again. All passions and interests have waned and there is nothing more we can think of that we might want.

There are also those who experience a great deal of grief during this period of a Void. All past losses that have not been fully experienced come to the surface, at last demanding to be fully felt with the mind and the body.

If the grief is due to losing loved ones through death, it can be especially painful. Attachment to people we are especially close to is a particular aspect of third-dimensional reality most of us have experienced. If we have deep attachment to loved ones who have died, the grief we feel may be too painful to endure at the time of death; and so it moves into our unconscious mind, along with other unfelt emotions.

We can live for years unaware of the unfelt grief. But with the Ascension process, it is bound at last to surface. It must be seen and at least briefly experienced before it can be released.

A friend of mine is living through a period in the Void like this, flavored with grief. After leaving the very busy life she'd lived for years, in which she was intimately involved with many people, she decided to move to Hawaii alone to just be with herself and the ocean.

Her time there has been rich with profound self-reflection and an experiencing of grief for multiple deaths of loved-ones she had never before fully allowed herself to experience. She speaks to almost no one and spends most of her time walking alone along the beach and swimming in the ocean.

I expect that at some point, she will know this period of Void is over and she will feel the draw to whatever might be next in her life. But meanwhile, she has simply given herself over completely to the process of death and rebirth, trusting that all is perfectly in order.

Whether it's grief, anger, depression, anxiety—or whatever other flavor we may be experiencing during our times in the Void—it's important to realize that at some point it will be time to let go of the emotions. We will know this when we become aware of a shift in ourselves. If we spend too much time after that dwelling on these emotions, or examining, analyzing, and trying to somehow fix them, we can effectively stop their release.

It's wise to neither resist an emotion nor distract ourselves from it. Consciously accepting it and allowing it to be present is important. But too much engagement with it after a point can also slow down its release, and we can end up recycling it through us over and over again.

It's helpful to remember that all the emotions that come up during a Void period are emerging for the sole purpose of leaving. The Ascension process demands it—these lower vibrations cannot continue to reside within us as we continue to ascend into a higher dimension.

Voids are Unavoidable

I believe these Void experiences are unavoidable in the process of Ascension. Spiritual awakening, as most of us know, involves ego dissolution—or more accurately, dissolution of our identification with the ego.

And as our identification with the ego along with all its concerns and interests evaporate, we begin finding we are no longer able to be "fed" by the people and activities that used to define our existence. As I've described above, reality can become a bleak desert of existential boredom in which nothing gives us any surge of fulfillment or significance.

The absence of feeling fed by what used to feed us usually isn't as difficult as some of our prior painful experiences in life; but we can still feel very far away from what we were hoping and expecting to happen as we began to fully awaken. At times we can feel as if we've somehow failed.

It's essential to understand that the emptied-out feeling is a crucial stage of awakening and to not attempt to avoid it by looking for new things outside of ourselves by which to be fed. I've often seen that when someone has reached this stage of the Ascension process, they panic at the emptiness and meaninglessness they are experiencing.

I notice that where they tend to go is in search of meaning through relationships. They either longingly seek a new love relationship, look for new friends, or attempt to resurrect relationships with family members that have grown stale due to their Ascension process into a higher vibration. These attempts, of course, prove futile in the end, as relationships in themselves are not able to feed us the manna we are now seeking—nurturance and freedom we can only find within ourselves.

This doesn't mean that our longing to be reunited with our true Soul family or community is misguided; we all deserve this companionship. It's just that to focus on this searching for new relationships or community can sometimes be a way of trying to avoid experiencing the despair of the Void that is usually necessary to experience in order to reach the next step in awakening.

When these times of desperation or despair arise, it's important to understand that it's a time to focus completely on surrender. I found that when I was able to do this while experiencing the Void, I discovered that inspiration and intuitive direction eventually began guiding me once again into a new and exciting direction. I simply needed to let go of all attempts to steer my way through the Void process, and instead let it simply have me.

I essentially came to the realization that there was no way out of experiencing the pain of the hopelessness and helplessness I was experiencing. And in doing this without either manipulation or avoidance, I would experience a sense of peace and see that my choices were then orchestrated by Divine Will, rather than my own.

But it was essential first that I give up every bit of hope or anticipation about outcome. I needed to completely trust that I would eventually somehow be lifted out of the despair and guided back into a direction of peace and well-being.

One of the most profound teachings I know is one that teacher Matt Kahn succinctly expresses as: "Whatever arises—love that." This is an important reminder for us in any stage of awakening we're in; but it is essential when we find ourselves in a stage of dissolution of ego identification. Only through acceptance and love for everything that arises within us, along with an intention to release what is not working, can we learn to step free of all our third-dimensional conditioning and despair.

Financial-Survival Challenges

Another difficult challenge I see a number of people in the throes of Ascension are facing is a financial-survival one. For some of us, this seems to be an important experience so we may truly learn about trusting the Divine to take care of us.

I myself had to find my way through one of these periods not long ago when my fears of survival arose in full force because my only steady and predictable income was suddenly being threatened. I realized I could quite suddenly be without any income; and since I was generally living hand-to-mouth and had no savings, I suddenly felt myself out on the dangerous precipice of survival.

I have actually been in this position a number of times in the past, as I seem to have brought in some definite poverty-consciousness karma this lifetime. However, I have always previously had at least a little something to back me up. Perhaps a small amount of savings, credit cards, or a house I could sell. Or the fact that I was a lot younger with more energy and passion about my work; or the economy was in much better shape and more work opportunities were available.

This time none of those things was in place. And additionally, my body was feeling old and tired. My mind could think of nothing at all I could do to quickly bring in steady income, and I couldn't imagine what other work I could possibly find or even how to go about looking for work during these times. The thought of having to go out and "market myself" to create a new counseling practice for which I no longer had a passion only left me exhausted. And I had no savings and no house I could sell.

And yet it was quite wonderful to watch how my tendencies to move into third-dimensional consciousness of panic and scrambled attempts to "solve the problem" didn't really happen. Somehow my studious practices in these past years to stay alert and to gently guide my mind into higher consciousness kept taking hold. Almost effortlessly, I found myself moving into trust and faith that I would somehow be taken care of.

I realized that through my efforts in creating this new groove in my consciousness toward higher awareness, the passage there had become deep and well-traveled. Fifth-dimensional consciousness of total trust had almost become my default consciousness. Going through this period of my life helped me to realize the progress I'd made along my path—and I have great gratitude for it. It showed me a water mark I'd created.

And, as might be predicted, a surprising new way to support myself did show itself, all in perfect timing. I was amazed. In the end, there was no reason at all for concern. It was clear that my faith that I'd be taken care of was based in truth.

I don't in any way feel special for having had this experience. I truly believe this can happen for any of us with enough faith in knowing we'll be taken care of, in one way or another.

Sometimes it takes a devoted practice in watching over thoughts and emotions stemming from poverty consciousness. But even when this is difficult, if we look honestly at our experiences, we will usually find we are always somehow taken care of—and sometimes in surprising ways. Out of the blue, new ideas occur to us, new doorways open; energy to begin an entirely different path arises. And sometimes money simply comes to us from totally unexpected sources.

Plateaus in the Awakening Process

From time to time another challenge I have faced in the Ascension process is feeling I've reached a plateau of some kind in which nothing much seems to be happening. After a period of either exciting new openings in consciousness or intensive clearing, it seems as if I've plateaued out and have somehow gone back to a previous unsatisfying "normal." I feel stuck. Many clients report this same experience.

I believe we all experience this at times. After periods of spiritual quickening and shifting, time passes and nothing more seems to happen. And so we just slip back, somewhat despondently, into living the life we were living before the quickening occurred. We may even forget about what has happened. Or perhaps we fall into feeling we've done something wrong, that we've missed a turn somewhere along the way, or we didn't focus or work hard enough to maintain the new awakening we'd experienced.

I believe these periods of plateau are generally periods of rest that are being given to us—periods designed for integration of all that has been occurring for us. It's important to be aware of this and not succumb to believing we've done something wrong simply because the intense or exciting shifts we've been experiencing have ceased for a while.

Fears of Awakening

On the other hand, if these periods extend too long and the feeling of stuckness continues, it may be that we are actually keeping ourselves from proceeding into deeper awakening due to fear. Consciously, of course, we do want to continue to fully awaken to who we truly are. However, we may have unconscious fears about this happening.

For instance, we may fear our own awakening because of how it might impact our relationships and our comfort around other people. Marianne Williamson speaks eloquently about this particular fear:

> "Our deepest fear is not that we are inadequate. Our deepest fear is that we are powerful beyond measure. It is our light, not our darkness that most frightens us. We ask ourselves, "Who am I to be brilliant, gorgeous, talented, fabulous?" Actually, who are you not to be? You are a child of God. Your playing small does not serve the world. There is nothing enlightened about shrinking so that other people won't feel insecure around you.
>
> "We are all meant to shine, as children do. We were born to make manifest the glory of God that is within us. It's not just in some of us; it's in everyone.

33

And as we let our light shine, we unconsciously give other people permission to do the same. As we are liberated from our own fear, our presence automatically liberates others."

Another fear a number of people are becoming aware of is a fear that if they fully awaken, something terrible will happen to them. From what I've seen in healings I've given people on this issue, many of us have had lifetimes in which we attained a high degree of awakening; and for whatever reason, we were either tortured, burned at the stake, imprisoned, or otherwise punished for expressing what we had come to experience. Thus the subconscious fear (although intellectually understood to be unfounded) is that this might happen again.

Another past life scenario that can play into the fear of awakening is one in which we may have awakened and then assumed the role of a spiritual teacher, prophet, or leader of some kind. And in that role we abused our power, bringing harm to others. Subconsciously, we fear being back in that position again and making the same mistakes.

I myself have had to face this fear over and over again. I've known I've had karma for abusing power in more than one lifetime. These memories have caused me to feel anxiety about moving forward into positions of power for fear of abusing it this time around, as well. With this fear, until recently, I somehow managed to sabotage every opportunity I was given to rise into a greater position of power and visibility in my life, subconsciously believing I'd be struck down and somehow punished.

There came a point in the last couple of years when I could no longer continue acting from this fear. I have simply kept moving forward into work that gives me ever greater power and visibility. But I do so with great care and a trust that I will maintain my integrity and commitment to assisting people in the best way I know how and not make the same mistakes I've made in the past. I've learned to hold a constant awareness of my motivations and actions.

"Fixing" Ourselves is Not the Answer

Even if we find it is fear that is keeping us stuck on a plateau, it's helpful to remember that moving back into a mode of attempting to fix ourselves is not the answer. There is nothing broken. There is nothing wrong with us. There is simply a deep fear sitting on the road in front of us, waiting to be met.

Effective Ascension work is different from how many of us learned to "work on ourselves" in the Third Dimension: through digging up the past and then re-experiencing the suffering and analyzing it in depth—all in hopes of somehow fixing and healing ourselves toward creating a sense of wholeness.

What works better in the Fourth Dimension is keeping a focus on what is already perfect and whole, and enhancing this awareness through being positive and compassionate with ourselves. An intention to focus on love is also very important. Just as remembering that loving all that appears in our lives is the most effective way to face the existential fear of emptiness that occurs in the Void, this approach is just as effective in addressing a fear of awakening, as well.

At some point we simply need to meet the fear head-on with trust and courage, feel it completely with acceptance and love—and see what happens. What we can usually discover is that the fear, being illusory at its core, dissipates and finally disappears. And we are left standing—not only unhurt, but stronger and more fearless than ever.

This process of facing fear may take a while and a number of sessions with ourselves before it totally dissipates. But it does work. It works because, in the end, we find that the fear is merely an ignorant third-dimensional reaction to an illusory threat.

Look at What Has Changed

There are times in the clean-out phase for a lot of us when it feels as if we've been moving through challenge after challenge in our Ascension process and yet nothing much seems like it has changed in our life to make it all worthwhile. I find it can be helpful to deeply inquire about whether this is actually true. I discover that if I do this, even when things may be tough or depressing, I generally find that much within me and my life has really changed for the better.

If you find yourself in that position, ask yourself: Aren't you more aware than you were two years ago—and not just a little more so, as might have happened in the past? Isn't there something inside you that is now stronger and more resilient? Don't you have a better understanding of what love is about—true, unconditional, spiritual love?

Think about it: Don't you have days in which joy just bubbles up in you out of nowhere for no reason at all? Or times, in the middle of great irritation or even despair, when you're suddenly inexplicably drawn into a profound inner peace? Maybe at times you're so filled with love, you're in tears?

And perhaps you're even having experiences in which you sense a karmic contract has just completed itself. Indeed, that maybe all karma in your life is coming to a close?

Many of us now walk around with a greater sense of inner peace. Less mind chatter. More self-love. More acceptance of life simply as it is. Greater detachment and ease. And more and more prolonged glimpses of utter freedom and knowing of who we truly are than ever before.

All these experiences are signs of Ascension, both the difficult and the wonderful. Occasionally these two types of experiences— joy-filled ones and painful ones—happen all in the same day, or even simultaneously.

Gratitude for the Challenges

Gratitude is yet another key for helping us through the clean-out phases we may be facing. At this point, just about everyone I know who is consciously moving along their Ascension path has been facing life-long emotional and physical challenges. But I see that it is those who keep focused on gratitude that make it through these periods with the greatest ease.

One person I know is finally facing a huge and solid energetic barrier she's felt around her all her life, one that has prevented her from ever truly feeling loved by anyone—and which has also blocked her from being able to effectively express her own love for others.

This has been gigantic for her to tackle; but with her knowledge about the period of Ascension we're in, she has been working with it, consciously facing and releasing all emotions, beliefs and memories that have created the barrier. It's unquestionably been hard work. I continue to remind her she doesn't need to fix herself—she simply needs to release all beliefs that something's wrong with her. When she gets this, she finds there's such joy she's experiencing, and such a sense of empowerment, that she has nothing but gratitude for it all.

A man I know is plowing his way through a fear of insanity he's had all his life; it has always been just below the surface of his awareness—but has more recently in his elder years reared its terrifying head. It's bringing up all sorts of serious physical symptoms with which he also has to deal. I've been in awe of the constant movement he makes over and over again into faith and a higher perspective of what's going on, as he handles both the physical and emotional challenges with a sense of thanksgiving.

Yet another friend has been dealing with multiple physical symptoms for a long while, with seemingly little progress in resolving them. Yet with her knowing that they are manifestations of when she had once abused her spiritual gifts and power in a previous life, she is dealing with them with a high level of awareness and understanding.

Very importantly, she's realizing that consistently only looking outside herself for help is not working. She must turn inward more constantly to hear the guidance available to her in order to handle the physical manifestations of the karma she's in the process of releasing. She too experiences great gratitude for the opportunity to learn all she is learning.

I have a client who is very consciously meeting the waves of karma in the realm of relationship that are washing over her with tremendous force. Very obviously, she's learning about the nature of love in the higher dimensions—and how different its expression is from what she's known in the Third Dimension. The understandings she's had are magnificent—but what she has had to endure and struggle through to come to them has been extremely difficult.

Over and over again, she makes her way through an intense situation and comes out the other side, feeling expanded, exhilarated and free now that she's made it through—just to turn around and find the next situation is upon her. She hardly has time to catch her breath.

But her willingness to pick herself up each time and continue on with clear intention is evident over and over again. Her longing for ongoing freedom and the ability to express love in a clear and powerful way keeps steadily moving her along. She too has expressed gratitude for her experiences. She knows she's gaining invaluable wisdom about the power of love. And her sense of gratitude has softened all the hardships she has endured in the process.

There are many important lessons those of us who are consciously working with the Ascension energies are learning about taking responsibility for what is happening in our lives. This includes not blaming anyone outside ourselves for the situations we're in; it also includes not falling into an attitude of blaming ourselves. It demands that we continually seek and hold a higher perspective about who and where we are.

It also calls for finding our way, over and over again, into our hearts and choosing both compassion and respect for ourselves. As we do all of this, a sense of gratitude can well up inside of us, helping us to experience the compassion and empowerment for which we long.

Learning the Higher Purpose

Yet another key for meeting emotional challenges during the Ascension process is to ask certain questions of our Higher Self, that aspect of ourselves that orchestrates the events in our lives to bring possibilities for learning, balancing karma, and awakening to our true nature.

The answers to these types of questions can give us information about the reason certain situations are happening in our life and what the goals are for us in meeting these situations. Rather than asking how we can fix a painful situation, change it, or make it go away, we can instead ask questions such as:

> ➢ Why is this situation being created for me?
> ➢ What am I invited to learn from it?
> ➢ What is the healing or transformation that can happen for me?

What we can realize with this approach is that nothing that is occurring in our life is random. Nor is anything a punishment. Everything being presented to us is offered through impeccable divine orchestration to provide an opportunity to learn, experience or transform something.

Each event, situation and relationship that appears in our life has been chosen with utmost care and presented in perfect timing. Nothing is casual. Once we get this, a profound trust can develop in us, a knowing that we are being led and guided carefully, with our full awakening always as the number one goal.

Chapter 4

Learning to Ride the Ascension Energies

As time goes on, I believe we are all discovering our own ways in which to ride the waves of Ascension energies that are flowing through us. Especially when we're experiencing clean-out, it's important to learn skillful ways that help us to stay in balance and on track.

I know people who are finding they need to slow down and curtail all their usual busyness. Others need to isolate themselves for periods of time. Still others are reaching out to friends and community to help them negotiate the rough waters in which they're finding themselves. Many of us are discovering that if we can learn to fully embrace every part of the transformation occurring within us, with faith—and, if possible, with passion as well—the ride becomes a lot smoother.

Ascension Symptoms

Virtually everything challenging we're experiencing due to our individual Ascension process can be seen as a symptom of Ascension. However, there are certain symptoms so many of us are experiencing that they are generally referred to as "Ascension symptoms".

I've found that there seems to be a wide range of these symptoms. What's interesting about them is they often seem to arise out of nowhere, with no obvious cause. And they also appear to come and go. At times they are symptoms we've experienced in the past. Other times, we can't even relate to them as something familiar; they just seem to be visiting us for a time and then they disappear.

With all of them, it appears they are symptoms of a shifting mind and body that are responding to the higher dimensional frequencies now flooding the earth. We are being cleaned out, releasing third-dimensional toxicity. Our thoughts and emotions are beginning to shift in vibration. Our many strands of long-dormant DNA are being reactivated. And our bodies are starting to morph into a less dense form, on their way to becoming crystalline light bodies that can function in higher dimensions.

In the following chapter we will look at the common physical symptoms people are experiencing due to the Ascension process. In this chapter we will explore those that are psychological. Our brains are being re-wired, old emotional patterns are releasing, and new energetic templates are being introduced into our bodies. It therefore comes as no surprise that we may go through emotional and mental upheaval at times, sometimes experiencing a number of different challenging emotions and thoughts on a daily basis.

Depression, Anxiety & Despair

The more common emotional ascension symptoms I hear about from people are depression and anxiety—and occasionally, despair. Often the feelings are somewhat mild and vague. But other times they can be deeply intense and debilitating. Almost always, they are relatively short-lived and seem to come out of nowhere.

These emotions are natural if we're experiencing the Void, as discussed in the last chapter. But even when that general feeling of being emptied out is not occurring, there are times when depression, anxiety and despair can appear.

I sometimes hear people say, "There's no reason for me to be feeling depressed. Nothing bad is happening. I just woke up this morning feeling it." The next time I speak with them, I hear that the depression just disappeared at some point.

I myself occasionally have days like this. I wake up in a strange mood of feeling anxious or depressed. I know that nothing has changed since the night before when I was feeling good. I usually decide that I'm in the process of releasing emotions that are coming up in my Ascension process, and I allow them to simply be present without giving them much energy. At some point they just seem to disappear.

Mood Swings

Another common psychological symptom people are experiencing is mood swings. It can sometimes feel as if we're "schizo", flip-flopping back and forth between moods, as the swings can be sudden and rather extreme. In one moment we can be feeling quite peaceful, expansive and optimistic about life. Then in the next, we're suddenly feeling depressed for no apparent reason.

Or we can be experiencing a warm and full heart at one point, loving everyone around us—only to be triggered by something someone says in the next moment and angrily reacting to them. We've dropped into 3D consciousness, totally forgetting the warm, heartfelt emotion we were just experiencing.

I have an old friend I've always experienced to be very steady, grounded, and remarkably stable in her moods. Lately, I never know what to expect. Each time we talk, she seems to be in a decidedly different mood from the last time we spoke. Sometimes she is very excited and cheerful about what is happening in her life. I love hearing all she tells me and always respond with enthusiasm and joy for what sounds like a new era in her life opening up. And then the next time we talk—sometimes the very next day—she is depressed, nearly in despair about her life.

When this first started happening, I was puzzled and somewhat alarmed. I was wondering if something was causing chemical changes in her brain. When I finally brought it up with her, she said she was aware of the rapid shifts in mood she was experiencing but that she didn't believe it was anything serious to be concerned about.

She explained that very uncomfortable issues and memories had been coming up for her, often out of the blue, causing her great pain and self-doubt. And that when she was dealing with them, everything in her life looked bleak and depressing. But then all the feelings would rather suddenly release, often in the sleep state at night, and she would wake up feeling optimistic and cheerful about her life again. What was startling was the rapid nature of the changes, as seemingly irresolvable "problems" would appear and then somehow disappear just as quickly.

We both realized what a poster child she was for the Ascension process. Her mood shifts were "normal" in this context—it's just how she was responding to the old energies coming up within her to be released—as well as to the new frequencies of the higher dimensions streaming onto the Earth.

Hypersensitivity

Something else I'm hearing often from people is the experience of becoming more and more hypersensitive. This can be an increased sensitivity to smells, sounds, light, chemicals and electromagnetic fields from technology. The sensitivity can sometimes be so extreme and disturbing to the nervous system that it's necessary to leave certain public places.

But what's even more common is a type of energetic hypersensitivity. As our vibrational level lifts and our sense of separateness from others decreases, we naturally absorb other people's energies more readily. And if these energies are of a much lower frequency than our own, it can become very uncomfortable to be around these people.

Many of us are empaths. It's wonderful to be naturally empathic with people. But, if we're not vigilant, we may feel ourselves automatically taking on other people's emotions and thoughts without even knowing it. Crowds in public places can be especially challenging, especially if there is a collective consciousness that embodies anger, fear or grief.

A number of us are also finding there are fewer and fewer movies and TV series we can tolerate. Even aside from the prevalence of violence in so many of them we can no longer tolerate, so much of what is depicted is about suffering of some kind—and it's increasingly difficult to watch beings suffer. If there is a redeeming feature such as a heart connection among the characters, or if true spiritual values are expressed in the film, we can maybe enjoy it—so long as it's not too sentimental, another quality we have less tolerance for, as well. Unfortunately, there is not much out there anymore with these qualities.

And then, of course, there's the mainstream news. This too is something many I know cannot tolerate anymore either. First of all, we realize that mainstream news sources can be sorely lacking in their accurate reporting of the news as well as giving actual disinformation. But it's also just plain too depressing to watch or read the news anymore. I actually feel a type of physical pain in my heart at times when I've been subjected to watching the news on someone's TV.

It's really important for those of us who are experiencing increasing hypersensitivity to set good boundaries around ourselves when we're out in public or if we're with individuals who are experiencing strong negative emotions. Surrounding ourselves with protective light is helpful, as well as holding a strong awareness and intention to maintain our own level of vibration.

We need to accept that simply leaving a situation that is pulling us down can also be an option. There is no advantage to anyone for us to feel uncomfortable or drained energetically. It's important to take responsibility for taking care of ourselves in this way.

Loss

Another common experience in the Ascension process is that of loss. It could be loss of relationships, sudden career changes, loss of financial support, or loss of one's home. Sometimes I find that people going through these kinds of changes see themselves to be failing at something or doing something wrong. They feel they're being rejected or punished; they're deficient in some way.

It's important to realize none of these things is true. The kinds of losses that are occurring in the Ascension process are simply signs of an unraveling life of ego identification. Our 3D lives no longer match our awakening consciousness.

The relationships and situations that are dissolving during this process represent the releasing of karmic ties to the vibration we once embodied when the circumstances or the relationships started. When seen this way, these losses can be understood as a "graduation" out of an outdated level of consciousness.

It's important when losses occur to not get lost in mourning what we've lost—but to rather focus on the greater possibilities the losses are creating for fuller, healthier, more awake experiences. If it feels too difficult initially to embrace the gift of the loss, then it can be helpful to focus on embracing the one inside us who grieves, with compassion, love and support. With this shift of our attention, the possibility of peace and acceptance can unfold—making way for an openness to the new opportunities that now await us.

Experiencing the Gift of Loss

A friend of mine recently went through the harrowing experience of fleeing her home due to a fire that raged through the entire community she had lived in for twenty years, completing destroying it. Except for a small suitcase of personal items and her computer, everything else she had owned was gone within minutes.

Her description of how she lived through the first few hours of that devastating loss left me awe-struck. She related that, as she drove down the mountain away from the fire along with many other evacuees, she was naturally in shock. But within the strange altered consciousness which shock can create, spikes of terror and grief would suddenly course through her, and her mind would automatically shoot into panic.

Yet thanks to many years of spiritual practice, she related that she found herself "on fire with awakening". She was fiercely awake, holding herself in the present moment like never before. Every time her mind would go into "If only...!" or "What am I going to do...?", she would immediately marshal her attention back to the immediate present and experience the fact that she was still alive and truly okay in the moment. Not an easy feat, but she determined to stay in that higher vibration and not allow the "facts" to alter her knowing that she was actually okay.

It's clear that she had accessed a fifth-dimensional state of consciousness and was choosing with firm intention to stay there, no matter what would continue to unfold in her life. It wasn't easy, and she had to continuously keep focused to avoid the pull of negative energies that were tugging at her. But, for the most part, she managed to succeed.

At the same time, in the ensuing days afterward she would suddenly experience times when profound grief and fear would arise and demand expression. She knew enough from past practice that it would do no good to try to hold these emotional surges down. She would therefore allow them to push their way through her body and let herself sob and moan for as long as the energy coursed through her. It was often just a few minutes before she felt it dissipate and release. She'd then relax into a profound state of peace. She found she was learning to ride the energies with full consciousness.

Two wonderful realizations have occurred for her through this experience. The first is how utterly free she now feels without all the "stuff" she had accumulated in her life. Her entire material life at this point fits into the trunk of her car. She not a young person who can easily live a mobile, transient life; she's in her late sixties and had accumulated throughout the years a number of things to create simple body comfort, health and ease. But she has realized that she can actually do without many of these things she'd felt were necessary. And the freedom she's experienced from this realization is extraordinary.

The second realization is how she has taken the huge loss in her life, with all it unknowns and inconveniences, as an opportunity to leap into higher consciousness. All crises offer us this opportunity, and if we look back in life to crisis situations we've lived through, we may see that we did take the opportunity to awaken to a higher level of consciousness through the experience.

But from what I can see, this friend has taken this opportunity to truly take a leap into fifth-dimensional consciousness. She is seeing clearly how anything is possible for her now. There are no limitations. She is sailing free and clear of many of the old structures of consciousness she's lived with her whole life. She is truly living a story of purification, one in which the phoenix is rising out of ashes.

As she moves through the world at this point, knowing nothing about where she will eventually "land" or how she will then live her life and continue to work, small miracles and synchronicities are a common occurrence. At every store or restaurant she goes into, people rush to give her everything she needs for free. They can't give her enough. And even the most reserved people feel the urge to hug her. I believe she is a beacon of light to many who may also eventually start experiencing loss as the dimensional-shifting energies continue to stream onto the planet.

So often life can feel like a random series of events that cause us to feel either fortunate or unfortunate. And the best we can do, if we're smart, is to learn how to meet every event with equanimity and acceptance.

But it becomes clearer and clearer to me that life is not a string of meaningless events. It is an intelligent and mysterious process that is divinely orchestrated for our growth and awakening. Every event, every relationship that shows up, every situation we find ourselves in—all is brought forward as a new opportunity to learn, to grow, to awaken more fully to who we are. There truly are no accidents.

And now more than ever I find that events that are happening to those of us on a conscious path of Ascension are exquisitely chosen and crafted by our Higher Selves to give us the next step we need to take to awaken as quickly as possible into fifth-dimensional consciousness.

If we can tune into this reality and take in the love that is being demonstrated through every situation that arises in our lives, we can experience an enormous sense of gratitude. And we can trust that loss of any kind at this point in our lives is truly a gift. If we can allow it, it will lift us into the very state of consciousness we have yearned for, for so long.

Boredom

There seem to be two types of boredom I hear about from people experiencing Ascension. The first seems to occur in the early stages of a Void experience, when someone is feeling that none of their usual interests, passions and creative outlets draws them any longer. They may try to resurrect these in different ways in hopes of stirring their interest again, but without success. There's just no juice left for what used to excite them.

This type of boredom arises from identification with the ego which is beginning to unravel; but identification hasn't shifted yet to a truer, more authentic self. So it's kind of a no man's land—one identity is dying (along with all its interests, passions and distractions), and nothing else is present yet to take its place at this point.

As I described earlier, for me this Void type of boredom could sometimes get grueling. There were times initially when my life had become so small and boring, I thought I'd go out of my mind. There wasn't anything I could think of that I really wanted to do in the time when I wasn't working, sleeping or eating.

I had been someone who had always had some kind of creative project going, and many different activities in which I was involved. All these had disappeared. I've got to say, I was so grateful to find movies and books I could tolerate so I could simply pass the time. With everything feeling so meaningless, it was good to have something at least to distract me for a while.

I know a man who has spent the last few years consciously moving through the clean-out phase of Ascension. For him, this has been a monumental endeavor, in that he spent a good part of his life since adolescence abusing alcohol and drugs and engaging in other unhealthy activities. His dedication to his healing process through all this is remarkable to me.

During this whole process, however, he has found that many aspects of his previous life have just fallen away—not just the parts that he was consciously leaving behind him—but also all interests and passions he once had that had made life exciting.

At one point, he found himself selling all his old equipment and tools that had been part of his former life and couldn't believe he was doing this. But he just couldn't find the enthusiasm he'd once had for the activities these things were a part of. He related to me that he now does next to nothing but meditate, say healing prayers, and surf the internet. He is not interested in almost any of his former friends or any activities in which he'd once been engaged.

Most of the time, he is cheerful and at peace with this situation. He believes his Soul purpose is to be a healer during these times of transition on the planet, but that the time hasn't quite arrived for this to happen. He understands that he is in a phase of the Ascension process that won't last forever. But sometimes he can go crazy with the boredom that arises during this time of waiting.

As difficult as it can be to live with this kind of boredom, if it's happening for you, know that you're on track. You're in transition from your third-dimensional identification into your fourth and fifth-dimensional identities. At some point, either new interests and activities will appear, or your old ones may reappear—but in a whole new way, because you will be different. The old ego agendas around the activities will have disappeared and your involvement and approach will be emanating from a deeper place, one more aligned with your Soul.

A second kind of boredom I'm seeing seems to come a little further down the path: It's a place in which everything in your life seems to be fine—but you discover that your emotional highs and lows seem to have disappeared. This can be especially apparent if you're someone who has generally experienced intense emotional highs and lows and have really enjoyed these dramatic moods.

What happens in this shift is a leveling out of the emotions. There's a calm peacefulness that pervades your mood. There's no real excitement or ecstatic joy, but no real depression either. And if you're used to emotional excitement or stimulation, it can initially feel rather boring.

But, as I experience it, it feels like living at a higher vibration. It feels steady and stable—and deeply peaceful. I can think clearly and stay present in the moment very easily, because so little is going on emotionally to distract me. It can just take some getting used to and appreciating.

Mind Attacks

There's another experience I've heard about from certain people that I can only label "mind attacks". This is when it feels as if your mind is going on the attack—or probably more accurately, your inner critic is. All you're aware of is a swirling mass of obsessive thoughts and emotions—judgments, blame, fear, anger, depression that arise and cycle over and over again.

This experience can be torture. It can feel as if you're trapped in your mind and can't get out. It's as if the ego is feeling its importance being diminished and is putting up a last valiant effort to pull you into its field of illusion through throwing all your most vulnerable issues at you at once.

I've found that the best way to handle this situation is to stop focusing on what the mind is throwing at you—and instead focus your attention on your body. Find the place in your body that is knotted up and put your hand on it. You'll find it's usually somewhere in the area of your gut, your abdomen or your chest.

Then start breathing as deeply and rhythmically as you can into this part of your body and focus on relaxing your muscles there— and then everywhere else in your body as well. Your mind will probably try to pull you back into its obsessive thinking. Just do your best to continue focusing on relaxing your body, and you'll find the power of the mind diminishing and finally letting go. There's something very primary about physical relaxation: when you're fully relaxed, it's very difficult for the obsessive thoughts and emotions to take hold.

Of course, another very effective way to calm the mind is to engage in some type of strenuous exercise, so that all your attention naturally has to move to your body. The vigorous exercise achieves the same result eventually: a relaxed body and a calmer mind.

Memory Loss

Many people I speak with tell me about the memory loss they're experiencing. It seems to be a common Ascension symptom, especially when it comes and goes. Sometimes it's what is called "delayed cognition", in which the brain takes longer to remember something than it used to. This is a typical aging symptom, but I hear even young people talking about experiencing it.

Rather than letting memory loss disturb you or send you into panic thinking it's a sign of dementia or Alzheimer's, try laughing at it. It actually can be very funny, especially if you're in a group of people who are all experiencing the same thing—attempting in vain to think of someone's name or the title of a movie they all loved but haven't a clue as to what it was called.

Of course, as with all these symptoms, if memory loss continues for a long time or becomes severe or debilitating, it may be valuable to consult a health practitioner about it. Always seek help from professionals if something is preventing you from living your life in a comfortable way. Even if it is simply a severe Ascension symptom that will eventually pass, if it's giving you too much concern or discomfort, find relief for it. Suffering needlessly does nothing to help us toward Ascension.

Disorientation

Many of us are experiencing a sense of disorientation at times, a disconnection from the environment and people around us. And sometimes it's a feeling even beyond disorientation: it's an experience of being in a totally strange and unknown land with an unfamiliar terrain. We feel as if we have no reference points anymore to what anything is, what's happening, how we fit in, or how we are expected to act.

I sometimes experience an even more primary kind of disorientation than one that is emotional or mental in nature—or even energetic. It has an existential and physical quality to it. As I walk outside in the world, I sometimes feel so disjointed in relating to both my body and the physical world, that questions come up like: "What is this that I am? And how does this fit into all the rest of what's out here?" Or "What is this strange thing called 'form' or 'physicality'?" I somehow can't relate to this aspect of reality anymore.

Another way to feel disoriented is when we're negotiating our way through two different realities at once. Inside of us, we may be feeling a sensation of joy and expansion, cruising along in 5D consciousness; and yet, at work or with certain friends, we're needing to act as if we're right there in 3D consciousness with them.

I have a friend who describes an experience she's currently having when she's with certain people that is rather amusing, but is also confusing. She says she finds when someone is speaking to her, she almost always knows how they're going to finish a sentence. It's all she can do to stop herself from either finishing their sentences for them or responding to them before they're finished speaking.

At the same time, since they're busy complaining about things in their lives, she's thinking she has to come up with things to complain about too, so they can feel a connection with her. And she has to scramble to come up with anything even resembling a complaint. "I don't know how to complain anymore!" she exclaimed, and we both broke up laughing.

It can sometimes get confusing and disorienting to continue pretending we're on the same wavelength with certain people. If we speak from an authentic place within ourselves, it can sometimes be alienating. They're either unable to relate to what we're saying, or they may even become hostile, if we're sounding too positive. So we fumble around, attempting to find something that might match their vibration enough to create a positive connection with them. It can get downright exhausting.

If you're experiencing any disorientation like this, remember that it's important to stay as grounded as possible. Go outside and be in nature, barefoot if possible. Or send an energetic grounding cord down into the earth. Also it can be helpful to get involved in something simple but pragmatic that needs to be done, like washing the dishes or balancing your bank statement.

Picking up Energy from the Collective

An even stranger Ascension symptom is the feeling that what we're experiencing doesn't even have anything to do with us. I sometimes hear people say things like "I feel like the anxiety doesn't have to do with me at all. It's as if I'm experiencing something from the collective. I'm just somehow connected to some group of people somewhere going through a rough time."

I believe this may be more common than we realize—that at least some of the negativity or fear that moves through us doesn't have anything do with us personally. We're simply tuned into an aspect of the collective consciousness—something arising either in groups we're involved with, certain groups of people across the planet, or the whole human collective. We're attuning to the experience of suffering or the fear the collective is feeling as it gets pulled by the Shift into a new and unfamiliar place.

There are times when I suddenly feel a sense of despair or anxiety out of nowhere. It has no context to it—it's just floating in me somehow. When I tune in, I realize the feeling is not personal. Nothing's going on in my own life that matches the feeling.

As I tune in more deeply, I find an energetic feeling of connection to a group of people, often across the world, who are likely feeling that despair or anxiety due to intense events happening where they're living. I'm not sure why I may be connected to them; all I know to do is to fill myself with love and send it to them, wherever they are. And with this, the feelings of despair and anxiety generally dissipate.

Whenever a friend of mine suspects she may be picking up something from the collective that is weighing her down, she uses a very simple but powerful consciousness tool offered by teacher Jim Self known as "The Rose". In this process she brings the image of a red rose into her inner vision and instructs it to magnetize all energies in her auric field that are not her own.

When she feels the rose has done this, she then instructs it to move into the air and explode or dissipate. If she feels better and clearer, she knows it was energies from the collective she was picking up; if nothing much happens she knows it was her own personal energies. It can be quite dramatic when low-vibrational energies seem to leave quickly.

We can also instruct the rose to protect us by enclosing us in our own energy field when we're with other people. And, further, we can instruct the rose to go out into the world where we've been and gather up all of our own energy we've left out there with other people and in other places and bring it back to us. It's an amazing little tool.

Pushed and Shoved and Stretched

Something else I personally experience at times is that I am being pushed, shoved and stretched endlessly by the Ascension energies. Sometimes it's simply on the emotional level. Other times, the experience may have more of a mental quality to it. Still others can be mainly physical—or a bit of all of these.

But always, when this feeling hits, it's as if I'm being compelled to take the next challenging step required without even a brief opportunity to gather and collect myself from the last effort or tumble. And I'm feeling stretched way out of my comfort zone.

Sometimes it feels as if I've had no break in time at all to simply relax or reboot. Often it's around feeling there's not enough time to do what I need to do. And other times the emotional or mental challenges present seem overwhelming, given what I'm feeling required to accomplish or endure.

At one point I complained to my guides about this: When was I going to get a break? When was I going to be able to relax before the next wave was going to hit me? What I heard in a very gentle voice was first of all an acknowledgment that yes, indeed, much was currently being thrown my way to accomplish, integrate, and recover from.

This acknowledgment was comforting to hear. But then I heard that the reason for my overwhelm was not actually all the stuff that was happening—it was the way in which I was responding to it.

Three Ways to Meet the Ascension Energies

Indeed, they said, there were three different ways in which I could choose to meet all that was happening. The first option was to continue what I was doing: attempt to keep control of everything, figure it all out, keep constant track of what I needed to do and when I needed to do it, and keep pushing my body forward. In other words, I could continue to try to stay in control of everything—and continue feeling pushed around and over-whelmed in the process.

The second option was to learn how to surf the wave of energy rather than feeling pushed by it: I could let go of trying to control it (which I couldn't, anyway—silly me for ever thinking I could). And instead, feel how the flow is moving and simply choose to align with it—and ride it.

I was assured that if I did this there would be no overwhelm. Everything I needed to do, experience, or say would be given to me in the moment it needed to happen. I wouldn't need to hold everything in my mind or try to keep in control of all I was doing.

"This all sounds good," I responded, "if I have the energy to do all this—to stay alert and ride the wave. But what about when I am so tired and brain-dead that I can't even do that?"

"Well, your third option is to choose to be *carried* by the wave of energy."

Letting the Ascension Energies Carry You

"Oh!" I exclaimed in hearing this, as a vision of a beautiful white chariot suddenly appeared in my mind, with a very comfortable chair resting securely within it. Out in front was a luminous Pegasus ready to carry me off into my life.

I stepped into the chariot and settled back into the chair—and off we flew. Soon I realized there were angels on both sides of me, helping to guide the chariot. What bliss! I was suddenly in tears, overcome with relief.

It was such a delicious experience—and has been each time I've used this image when I have felt in overwhelm, either about not enough time, not enough brain cells to remember things, or not enough stamina and energy to make it through whatever is going on.

And during those times when I do have energy and a clear mind, I practice surfing the wave. I've discovered that this can be such fun—sensing where the wave is taking me, all the twists and turns, and moving with it. And what a thrill to ride an energetic wave of such force—not needing to know where it's taking me, simply trusting it's where I need to go.

The amazing thing is realizing that what I was told is true: I can just let go of trying to remember things I need to do at certain times. Over and over again, right when I need to remember something, I am reminded. Everything flows and emerges, all in right timing.

Psychic Attacks

There is one last Ascension symptom I wish to describe. It's one I have felt reluctant to include in that it points to negative forces outside ourselves and can instill fear. It is also not a common one for most people, although it may be more common than any of us is aware of.

But I am urged to include its description here, because lightworkers who are becoming visible to the world through their work do occasionally experience this Ascension symptom and it can be helpful to recognize it and know how to deal with it. It's known as a "psychic attack."

These are times when anxiety, depression, despair—and even terror—can seem to appear out of nowhere and roll through us in great waves. And they don't pass through as easily as other Ascension symptoms do.

These intense episodes may simply be experiences of something traumatic we endured at some point in our life (or perhaps in a past life) that we were unable to fully experience and integrate at the time and it is now suddenly coming up to be experienced and then released.

Or they may be experiences in which we are dealing with disincarnate entities that have entered our auras and are wreaking havoc with us—especially now as we begin waking up into our own power. I work with a surprising number of people who seem to be dealing with this phenomenon described as "possession" at this point in their Ascension process. I write more about this phenomenon in Chapter 10.

But the third explanation of intense episodes can be what has been named "psychic attacks". These are emotional and sometimes physical attacks by entities or energies that haven't necessarily attached to our aura, but can go after us simply because we are expanding into an ever-greater light consciousness and are becoming more "visible" on the inner planes.

I myself have had two such experiences for which I have no conclusive explanations—except that they were extraordinarily intense and had no apparent reason for happening.

A Story of Terror

About four years ago, I went through an entire week in which I was fortunate if I got even two or three hours of sleep each night. A very strange thing would begin happening every evening as night time approached: an irrational terror would suddenly emerge and grip me—and it would not let go. There was no reason I could think of for any feeling of fear about anything in my life at that point. It made no sense.

But it was as if, once night came on, this terror would emerge from the depths of my being—rather like a gigantic dark creature from the black lagoon surfacing inside me and howling with an ungodly shriek. And I would be clutched in the grips of this creature, sitting paralyzed for hours, unable to think or know what to do but simply experience the terror.

It was interesting because, even once morning would appear during this whole week, and the creature seemed to submerge itself again into my unconscious again, I never thought to seek help for making it through the next night when I knew it would arise within me again. Somehow I knew this was something I needed to experience and make my way through alone.

By the third day, however, I was fortunate in finding a possible explanation for what was happening. I was glancing through Adyashanti's *The End of your World*, a wonderful book I'd already read and totally related to. But there was a section I opened to that I'd thought I'd understood when I'd first read it—but now realized I hadn't. And it seemed to possibly be explaining what I was experiencing.

It was the section in which he describes what he calls "awakening at the level of the gut". He describes how a profound irrational fear exists at the core of our being that is experienced in the area of the gut—exactly where I was experiencing it. He explains that during the process of awakening, this fear must be met—and it must be met with total surrender. This was the approach with which I felt I had been attempting to meet the terror, and I determined to continue focusing on this same approach that night.

And indeed, I was better ready for the deep-sea creature's emergence that evening. As night-time fell, sure enough, up it came as terrible as ever. As before, my entire gut clutched in terror. But this time more of my awareness was present and with greater strength. I knew I simply needed to be with it, surrender to it, and let it have me. And I managed to do this with some success. I was just enough in charge of my reactions to be able to choose to consciously surrender.

The night passed once again with my not being able to do much more than just sit experiencing the terror, surrendering to it. But there was greater awareness present, and a sense of power I felt in meeting it.

During the following few nights, this awareness and power grew steadily as I met the creature. By the seventh evening, I had gotten to the point finally at which I was actually boldly calling to the creature to come on out. I was ready for it. It was not going to destroy me; I knew this now.

And sure enough, when it did appear I could see that its power had totally waned. I was no longer paralyzed by it. I had withstood its attack and was no longer feeling frightened by it. And within an hour or so, it was as if it just slipped away in defeat. I was able to sleep well that night. And it's never appeared again.

At this point I'm not clear whether this experience was actually what Adyashanti was describing. With hindsight and greater understanding about the phenomenon of psychic attacks, I realize this experience may have actually been an attack—and not a "normal" experience in the process of awakening. But either way, it didn't really matter. My approach to it seemed to be a powerful and effective way of handling it, whatever it was.

A Story of Despair

A few years later, I had another strange experience—similar in one way to the sea-creature episode, but different in flavor. This one began with about a week of a sense of meaninglessness continually wafting through my consciousness.

The questions kept coming to me: "Why even get up in the morning? For what? Nothing means anything. And there's so much suffering in the world. Why does anyone keep on going? There's so little joy or pleasure to compensate for it all."

This feeling of depression and these kinds of questions were not unfamiliar to me. Many times throughout my life I'd experienced the existential despair of a lack of meaning in anything occurring in life. At one point as I experienced this in earlier years, I became aware that objects, situations, and experiences don't actually have any inherent meaning to them; it is we who assign meaning to them. Paradoxically, this realization would give me solace, and the sense of meaninglessness would fade.

But this understanding did nothing for me during this one week. Again, there was no apparent reason for this to be happening at this point in my life. Nothing out of the ordinary was happening. In fact, life was pretty good; I was feeling quite content and even joyful about certain events that were occurring.

Yet the sense of meaninglessness kept grabbing at me, bringing on a vague feeling of despair with it. I kept on top of it, so to speak, not allowing it to take over. It just required vigilance, and a consistent thought that it was probably just another Ascension experience of ego dissolution.

Although somewhat uncomfortable, the whole experience was mild enough during the week—until the seventh night of it. I was in the middle of what was usually a rather pleasant task—making some great sugar-free cookies I loved. Suddenly, out of the blue, it was if a strangle-hold sensation of despair gripped me. It was so intense, I dropped my spoon and just stood there clutching the counter in shock.

As I say, it's not like I was a stranger to despair. I had felt this many times earlier in my life, and had managed to survive thoughts of suicide during several of these times. But back then, there were always reasons for the despair—events or situations in my life that felt unbearable. At this moment in my kitchen, there was nothing like that present. There was just despair so intense that death was the only solution I could think of that would make the experience vanish.

Fortunately, I had just enough presence of mind to call in the Holy Spirit for assistance. I couldn't think of any of the other powerful spiritual tools I knew that I'd normally use in situations in which I'd need help—but this one came to me and I used it.

But I could barely feel the presence of the Holy Spirit. I just stood there as the despair gripped me for about five minutes. And then it just suddenly released. I sat down, recovering from what had definitely felt like a psychic attack.

However, I wasn't sure. As I explored inside myself, I was quite sure there was no actual entity with me. But maybe dark energies were present and had been attacking me. I could kind of feel their presence around me, but receding. Or was it just something very dark within me that needed to be released?

As I say, it doesn't really matter what these kinds of experiences actually are. What does matter is how we learn to meet them. Often while we're in the experiences, there is seemingly no room for awareness to exist; there is only the meeting of the "demon" in whatever form it attacks us.

But it is in the simple meeting of it that we gain more power and awareness. And it's in the surviving of it that we emerge strangely enriched with deepened understanding and greater empowerment.

I believe not many of us are experiencing these kinds of attacks; but for those who are, it is helpful to be aware of what they may be. It behooves all of us lifting rapidly in consciousness to consistently surround ourselves with light and to take other protective measures when we go out in public.

And especially if we are healers, therapists, or health practitioners, it's important to be aware of the invisible levels of energy with which we may be dealing and to clear our auras as best we can after any encounter with a client or patient.

The Waves Come and Go

I have enough experience now to know that the waves of Ascension that wash through us during difficult periods come and go in our lives at this point on the journey. And often there are resting times in between them in which we can relax and integrate what we've been experiencing, releasing, and learning.

We can take the time during these quieter periods to fully experience the new feelings of clarity, lightness, balance and fulfillment that are flowing in, in the aftermath of the receding energetic wave that crashed into our life.

Ascension isn't for sissies. And those of us who have chosen to make the shift into the Fifth Dimension consciously, knowing we've volunteered to assist others in the process, seem now to be experiencing an ever-increasing force of change and movement in our lives.

How fortunate to know there are different ways in which we can meet the challenges—and that they don't all have to be hard!

Quick Keys for Handling Ascension Stress

There are some other keys I've learned that are helpful in handling the stress of the Ascension process—measures that are quick and relatively easy to remember.

Deep Breathing

Be careful not to dismiss this idea with a quick "Oh yeah, I know about breathing." You may well know the importance of it—but you may also tend to forget to keep aware of your breathing and the importance of the relaxation it brings.

It's especially important to remember the power of breath when you're under stress or filled with fear, the times you generally stop breathing. Deep breathing releases muscle tension which has been shutting off blood to both your body and your brain.

Focusing on breathing during these times of stress is one of the most effective ways to bring about a sense of calm and power. It grounds you and helps you to think clearly. Take in deep, rhythmic and continuous breaths. You'll find that you can't breathe deeply and keep tense at the same time. And as you let go of the muscle tension, you can find that you're not only relaxing, you're slowly becoming able to think more clearly, as well.

Present Time

No matter what's happening, remember that you can always meet it most effectively and with the least amount of pain if you bring yourself into the present moment and experience yourself there. We create most of our anxiety by moving into the future in our minds. And most of our grief by focusing on the past.

We have no control over either the future or the past. They aren't even real, except as thoughts in our mind. We only truly have the present moment—and our choice of how to meet what is happening in that moment.

Surrender

When you find yourself attempting to control a situation or stop it from happening out of anxiety—and you're not having any success—surrender. Consciously make the decision to give up all your efforts to control anything. Take a deep breath and let go of any pushing inside you, any pressure to make something happen. Allow and accept what-is.

Conscious surrender isn't a helpless decision to resign yourself to fate; it's a purposeful decision to flow with whatever's happening—and to trust that the situation is taking you where you need to go. It's a surrendering to the Divine plan for you.

It's Releasing

Keep remembering that whatever is arising within you—all challenging emotions, memories, and limiting beliefs—are arising in order to be released. They're not there to invite engagement or struggle. This is especially true with issues you've dealt with and attempted to heal for years. Don't move into resisting them or denying them; but don't try to process them either or go over them one more time.

They're on their way out for good. Let them go, release them. Greet them with the energy of "Hello—thank you—goodbye!"

Living Words

One of the most powerful tools I've learned through the Mastering Alchemy program offered by Jim Self is one I use to quickly shift my experience of something challenging occurring in my life. It entails repeating certain positive, high-vibrational words to myself. There is a wide variety of words that have an especially potent effect on me when I simply say them to myself and then pause to feel them, such as "happy", "well-being", "gratitude", "commanding", and "ease".

This sounds so simplistic, and yet it is surprising how quickly my whole perspective on something changes when I do this and how profoundly my emotions and thoughts shift. This is because all words carry vibrations with them, and we are automatically affected by our use of them, both silently and out loud. Certain body states are naturally called forth when hearing or speaking words, along with memories of when we've felt the meaning of them.

It's very simple to test this for yourself. Choose a state of being (either an adjective or a noun works) and repeat this word to yourself a few times. "Happy" is a good one to begin with. As you say the word, feel into your body for where this state of being resides and shift your awareness there. You'll see that saying the word causes the feeling to arise. In fact, it's difficult to say the word over and over to yourself and not feel a smile appear on your face.

As the feeling of "happy" arises within you, pause to rest in it for a few moments. Experience it deeply. The more you do this simple process with any word you'd like to experience, the faster the state of being appears and the easier it is to fully immerse yourself in its energy.

You can also create a "word triangle" to use when you're about to enter a new or difficult situation—or to set a tone for an entire day—by choosing three words that create a more complex state of being. For example, if you are about to walk into an interview you feel nervous about, you might choose "self-confidence", "ease", and "success". Or if you're feeling tired and you're about to enter a situation in which much energy will be required of you, you might choose "vitality", "strength", and "energy".

It can help to see the three words in a triangle configuration—one word at each corner of the triangle or along its sides—and repeat them to yourself in a relaxed but focused manner. Feel the words elicit the corresponding body and emotional experiences in you.

Using this simple tool can profoundly change your life, as the practice begins to short-circuit old habit patterns of negative thinking and the related emotions the thoughts create. New neurological pathways are forged within you, and after a while it becomes natural to experience these higher vibrational states of being.

Laughter

One of the most effective and enjoyable ways to break a stress cycle is to find humor in something happening and to start laughing. If you're with other people and they can catch the humor and start laughing as well, it can become a most enjoyable cathartic experience for everyone involved.

Sometimes a fit of laughter will eventually bring on a spell of crying. Allowing tears to flow for a while can also be helpful in relaxing the stress in both your mind and your body.

Be careful to note, however, when you have accomplished this. You can feel when the energy has been released—there's a pause and a sense of relief. If you then decide to continue crying out of a sense of self pity, you'll find it will not be beneficial to you. You'll just be pulling the sadness and stress back into your body.

Physical Exercise

Another well-known remedy for handling stress is vigorous exercise. It can feel overwhelming at the times when you're feeling stressed to even think of getting up to get some exercise. But once you do pull yourself up and decide to do it, it can be an amazing experience to see how well it works. Your attention is drawn into the present moment as your body begins moving, and there isn't room for muddling around in your stressed-out mind.

Afterwards your body can feel so much better—and you find your mind is clearer and more able to problem solve about whatever was causing your stress.

Love Yourself

Above all, during any of your difficult times, remember to love and accept yourself just the way you are. Be kind and compassionate to yourself at these times. The Ascension process is not easy for anyone. It's a daunting adventure into the Unknown, often leaving us bereft of any of our old reference points of how to function in our lives. Loving yourself through it all can make anything you're experiencing easier—and also get you to where you're going faster.

Chapter 5

The Body's Ascension Process

It's clear there's a great variety of Ascension symptoms that are of a psychological nature. There are also symptoms that are mainly physical, and they come in many varieties, as well.

Physical symptoms should especially come as no surprise to us, if we understand that our physical body is in the process of transforming itself into a crystalline body of light to hold our emerging fifth-dimensional consciousness. We are undergoing immense cellular transformation that is accelerating our very atomic structure.

Biological Upgrades

This quickening is impacting every system in our bodies and working them overtime, releasing toxins from the physical, emotional and energetic levels. In addition, our bodies often don't get much time to recalibrate, as they're also attempting to adapt to the new frequencies flooding the earth. We're receiving, in essence, a huge biological upgrade, and in a very short period of time.

So many changes occurring in our bodies can temporarily weaken our immune systems at times, setting us up for possible infection and inflammation. Our endocrine systems are also moving through a significant upgrade, which can create tremendous energy shifts and overloads. Glandular activity can become erratic, causing an impact on our body chemistries. All of this, in turn, can create both adrenal and mental depletion, giving rise to confusion, exhaustion, disorientation and depression, as well as a variety of additional physical symptoms.

As might be expected, those of us with older bodies seem to be most impacted physically by the Ascension process. Our bodies have been in the process of aging for a while and have had more years of stress on them. And if we are Souls who have been incarnating on this planet in the Third Dimension since very ancient times (and many of us have), we have also typically brought a load of karmic patterns in with us this time to balance, much of which has found its way into our bodies.

I have also found in my work that there are others who have come to this planet rather recently from distant galaxies, and they carry DNA in their bodies that is quite different from "normal" human DNA. Doctors and other health practitioners often have difficulty in understanding their bodies. These people, too, are experiencing unusually difficult challenges with their bodies that are attempting to make the transition from 3D to 5D.

Common Physical Ascension Symptoms

The list of common physical symptoms many of us are experiencing is long and varied and depends on the personal history of body insults we've experienced, our genetic weaknesses, and our particular constitutions. However, some of the most frequently-reported symptoms, most of which seem to come and go and have no certain known cause, include:

- ➢ headaches that shift around the head
- ➢ unusual pains and aches
- ➢ sleep problems
- ➢ digestive difficulties
- ➢ reappearance of old injuries
- ➢ joint pain
- ➢ sensation of electrical shocks in the head, body or field
- ➢ fatigue

Nervous System Recalibration

An odd symptom that can also show up from time to time is an internal type of shaking that stems from the recalibration of the nervous system. This results from our energy field adjusting to the increasing absence of the negative and limiting cellular memories we've carried in our bodies for so long.

We might interpret this internal shaking as anxiety or fear—or even as anger or frustration if the emotional distress is projected outward. But it's really just an internal energetic reorganization that's occurring. I've found that when it starts happening, the best thing to do is to sit still and focus on taking deep, slow, measured breaths, until the shaking eventually subsides. Of course (as with all of these Ascension symptoms), if it continues for a time and there is concern, it is wise to seek medical attention to make sure it is not something more serious.

"Ascension Flu"

Then there's the experience that seems to be quite common called the "Ascension flu". This includes feeling achy all over, fatigued, feverish and headachy—with the addition of possible digestive and sleep difficulties. I tend to see this phenomenon as similar to a typical detox situation or "healing crisis" that can happen after we've first engaged in a new physical healing modality. This occurs primarily because we're in the process of releasing old emotional patterns, and they've gotten caught in the body and need to be released at that level.

People I work with sometimes have this experience after a healing I've given them, especially if it's been an especially profound healing. They are generally people who are very eager to move through their issues quickly and get through to the other side of the healing as fast as possible.

And what they end up doing is biting off more than they can comfortably chew. In their impatience to heal an emotional issue, they plunge into their emotional releasing with such enthusiasm that their bodies begin detoxing very quickly, causing them a great deal of discomfort. As many of us know, there can be too much of a good thing.

I myself have been guilty of doing this. I can get impatient or simply over-eager to use an energetic clearing tool of some kind, and I'll bring on too much clearing at once. There have been times, in fact, when I have experienced a number of different parts of my physical body suddenly giving out all at once because I have stressed my endocrine system this way.

However, I've noticed that my response to my body's uncomfortable healing process has really shifted over the last few years. My former tendency would have been to get anxious, feeling that my body was finally really getting old and was on its way out.

But most of the time these days, I have been quite pleasantly surprised at my general response to my body's ailments. Although I have definitely experienced some initial spurts of fear in which my mind starts down the familiar trail of panic and feeling sick and alone, these reactions never seem to last long.

If I stay alert, I can shift rather quickly into a higher consciousness, knowing there is something larger at play, that something is arising and moving through me in order to be released. I know that my physical body is where emotional and mental trauma that has not been fully experienced and released in the past (for who knows how many lifetimes) has eventually lodged. And this is how I'm holding these episodes now.

I do my best to focus with great love and appreciation for my body during these times. And I also keep aware that greater freedom, wisdom and strength are awaiting me at the end of it. I know these are passages I am going through that have purpose. And with that knowing I can experience enormous gratitude along the way for the awareness I have of the Ascension process.

Exhaustion, Sleep, and More Exhaustion

Perhaps the most common physical symptom I hear about from others is exhaustion and the need to sleep many more hours than usual—and then not feeling any more refreshed, even after sleeping. I've had to deal with this myself at times. There have been days when I could barely drag myself from my bed to my chair.

For some people, of course, actual illness (such as Lyme Disease, an increasingly common disease these days) may be responsible. But, as with other Ascension symptoms, I'm not convinced that this ongoing and debilitating exhaustion can be explained away just by the usual medical reasons. Often we have no other flu-like symptoms, nor is there anything unusual going on in our lives that might cause exhaustion.

My sense is that it is a response we are having to the Ascension energies streaming into the earth from the highly unusual solar activity that's occurring and from other places even deeper in the galaxy. Often, too, many of those describing their exhaustion to me are moving through some very deep, and often unconscious, issues in their lives. Some of the issues have been central throughout their life and may also be residue from previous lifetimes.

Energetic Exhaustion

Something I've personally been aware of in my own body is the distinction between exhaustion which feels essentially physical or mental-emotional—and one that's more energetic in nature. Energetic exhaustion seems to include exhaustion of my physical, mental and emotional bodies, but it also extends into much deeper levels of my being. It especially seems to hit me on the energetic or etheric levels within the very cells of my entire endocrine and nervous systems.

I became aware of this level of exhaustion recently when I woke up one morning after an extremely powerful healing and realized I was experiencing a deep relaxation throughout my entire body I hadn't experienced for years. Absolutely every fiber in my body felt cleaned out and relaxed.

I realized that what was missing was the sensation of energetic stress. And that what I was now experiencing went far past muscular relaxation and relaxation of my mind and emotions: it felt like a relaxation within every cell, as if I'd gone through a cellular "car wash".

Those of us in the healing professions really need to watch for this kind of exhaustion. As empathic individuals, it's easy to unconsciously take on low-vibrational energies from the people we're working with that add to the challenges our bodies are already experiencing.

Time to Slow Down

Aside from telling us we're in Ascension mode, what else might our exhaustion be pointing to? One thing to notice is that many of us are simply having to slow down—and in some cases, actually stop, all our doing. Exhaustion forces us to arrange our lives so that we can simply make it through a day without a lot of mental activity or physical stress.

Exhaustion also compels us to pay attention to more of the details of how we live and to focus more closely on our body's needs. Rather than paying so much attention to what's going on "out there", we find we need to keep our attention more closely on what's happening within ourselves in the immediate present.

Fortunately this tendency to keep more of our attention on ourselves can be a much needed shift of focus for some of us. Perhaps we have been too focused on all our activities, all that we feel we need to get done. Maybe we've been pushing ourselves and have been losing touch with our bodies and what we're feeling. Perhaps we've just been doing too much, too fast, and haven't taken time to integrate all the inner changes we haven't been conscious of.

It could be that we're simply being encouraged to experience more BEing and less doing. Instead of trying to get in another hour of work or socializing, perhaps we could sit somewhere in nature and experience becoming one with the trees, the wild flowers and the breeze. Just slow everything down and truly be present in the moment.

One thing, however, I find really fascinating is that, even on days when there are a number of things I really do have to accomplish, I find I *can* complete everything I have planned to do with relative ease, even while moving very slowly. It's a matter of staying totally present in the moment, completely relaxing and focusing on that with which I'm currently engaged. As soon as I start leaning forward into the next activity or into thinking about all I need to accomplish, I feel overwhelmed. I just want to close my eyes and fall asleep.

But being present with myself in a gentle and compassionate way seems to actually give me energy. It also somehow seems to make time stretch. I am amazed at how slowly time then passes and how much I can accomplish. This, I know, is the key to functioning in fourth-dimensional time. The sensation of time passing too quickly is something I experience only when I'm functioning from a limited third-dimensional consciousness.

Stilling the Critical Voice

Dealing with exhaustion can also be an opportunity to hear an inner critical voice telling us about ourselves. I've found almost across the board with those dealing with exhaustion that they've become aware of the repetitive critical messages they're hearing in their heads about their exhaustion, telling them that something must be "wrong" with them. It's telling them they've done something wrong to cause the exhaustion and they need to "fix" it.

Speak about adding fuel to the exhaustion! Self-criticism alone can cause it.

If we're listening to our inner critic voice, it's important to question what it's telling us. We will likely find there are beliefs it reveals that we may be taking as truths. Like "I shouldn't just sit around and do nothing. I'm not okay if I don't accomplish something today."

It's valuable to ask: "Are these statements actually true? Do I know that productiveness is inherently better than just sitting around doing next to nothing? Or is this just a belief?"

Or how about: "If I'm this exhausted, I need to figure out why. I need to do something to fix it. There's something wrong if I feel exhausted. There's something wrong with me".

Is this true? Do we know this for sure? Or is this an assumption we have, based on what we may have learned early on in life from our parents or the culture around us—or even from some third-dimensional religious or spiritual teaching?

Exhaustion can even be seen as a good thing. It could be feedback from our body telling us something important about not just our physical health, which is important enough—but also about what may be necessary in our awakening process.

We can't know until we question these beliefs. The important thing is to recognize the beliefs as beliefs, and then test them to see if there is any truth in them.

Exhaustion and Depression

I've found that another pathway people often take when they're feeling physically exhausted is to assume they're feeling depressed. Exhaustion can feel like depression. And of course depression may be part of it: if we don't have the energy to do the things we usually enjoy doing, this may feel depressing. But the actual exhaustion isn't necessarily a depression.

If we try pushing ourselves to accomplish all our usual activities while feeling exhausted, that can certainly bring about a feeling of depression. But if we can stop pushing ourselves and take time to carefully consider what we absolutely have to do during a day, it can be helpful. Then we can choose to move slowly, staying present with ourselves in the moment.

I've discovered that when I'm exhausted, I can be aware that I'm simply moving in slow motion. I'm conscious of every movement I'm making, and I'm staying present in an immediate way with myself. I'm resting when I need to. And I'm experiencing a deep stillness in my mind. Life becomes a moving meditation.

In this slower mode, I also begin to notice small details around me that I might normally miss—like the beauty of a tree outside the window, and the squirrel that just jumped onto a branch. I become aware of the sweet tenderness that enters my heart as I witness this.

Insomnia

Although many of us report having an increased experience of sleepiness along with exhaustion, not all of us are able to get the sleep we need due to chronic insomnia. At times the insomnia is explainable: there are issues surfacing that keep us awake and often there are feelings of depression or anxiety involved.

But sometimes there are no apparent reasons for the insomnia. Many people I work with are reporting this. Some have had sleep disorders for a long time; but the inability to get enough sleep at night—even while taking sleep aids—seems to be more prevalent now than ever. I myself move in and out of periods of insomnia and it can be extremely frustrating.

The main thing I try to remember is to not add the energy of frustration or anxiety about my inability to fall asleep to the already-uncomfortable effects of my insomnia. Staying as calm as possible during the period of middle-of-the-night awakeness is important for both eventually falling back asleep and for not feeling exhausted in the morning. Reading, meditating or doing simple chores around the house helps. And avoiding bright lights and the computer is essential.

And meanwhile I remind myself that this will not be forever. Everything is in transition. Everything is shifting. When I listen deep inside me, I know there will come a day when all will come into balance in both body and mind.

Our Bodies are Trying to Catch Up with Us

The main thing we need to remember is that our physical bodies are very dense third-dimensional vehicles. Often they have to adapt to keep up with our quickly evolving consciousness and the recalibrations and upgrading happening within us.

If we could simply evolve without our physical bodies, it might be a lot easier. But this game of Ascension we've signed up for apparently includes taking our bodies into the much more subtle energetic fields of the Fifth Dimension.

Much has to shift in the denseness of our bodies. And when a lot of change and rewiring is taking place, our bodies very naturally need to rest and reduce their energy output so other processes can function optimally.

It's clear we need to be compassionate toward our physical bodies as they haltingly attempt to follow our consciousness through this unusual course of evolution. We need to take time to ground ourselves and allow for recalibration.

For some of us, impatience can arise when we're moving through a process of healing. We can feel as if we want to fast track the healing process and just get it over with. I've found personally and seen with a number of clients that this attitude doesn't work well. If we try to accelerate the healing in our bodies in any way, our symptoms may get worse. But if we dare to slow ourselves down to honor the healing taking place and allow for the time our bodies need, the healing is a much smoother process—as well as faster in the long run.

We also need to keep in mind that if we are to do the work we're here to do, we must have strong and fortified bodies. We therefore need more rest and times in which we can simply BE. We can also probably use more periods of play, something rather foreign for many serious-minded people in the throes of Ascension.

We would also do well to keep our bodies in an alkaline state, and keep our lives as stress-free as possible. We can make healthier choices in food and consider supplements to fortify and re-build our immune systems.

And if there are days when all we can manage is resting, sleeping, and doing nothing more than taking care of our bodies, so be it. What are our priorities, after all? Having a busy life with a lot of distractions—or our journey into our next step in evolution?

Energetic Tools for Healing Our Bodies

I have discovered a couple of very simple yet effective ways to bring healing to my body on the energetic level. I've actually been rather stunned a few times when I've used these techniques at how effective they are.

Golden Liquid Light

The first is to call in golden liquid light through the crown chakra and slowly pull it down through the body until every cell is bathed in it. See each cell receiving this light and being cleansed of all impurities, both physical and energetic—and then left sparkling clean, with new vitality and energy.

You can bring the light systematically through each system of your body, or simply draw it into all parts of it as the light travels down. Or you can focus on one particular organ or gland. Visualize the light melting into the earth once it's drawn through each cell or part of your body.

You can also add divine love—or your own love—to this light as an extra ingredient. In my experience our bodies respond instantaneous to love.

Whenever I do this process on myself, it's as if my cells are eagerly opening themselves to the light when they're being bathed in it, drinking it in and sighing with comfort and relief. I can feel a tingling in my body afterwards, along with a deep sense of well-being. If there has been pain in some part of my body, the pain is often significantly alleviated.

Tender Cradling

Another method I've learned came to me one day out of the blue. I had been dealing with problems with my colon, doing everything I knew to do on the physical level. I had also been bringing light to it daily, which seemed to help significantly. But it was slow going.

Then one day when I closed my eyes, thinking about my colon, I was suddenly shown an image of myself cradling my colon in my arms, as I might a young baby. I was startled by this image at first, but then it brought tears to my eyes. I realized that this was the energy my colon was desperately needing—a tender, gentle love.

I moved into the image and felt myself pouring love into this colon in my arms, stroking it and gently massaging it. As I did this in my mind, I could feel my actual colon responding. Something seemed to settle it and a new calm flowed through it.

Since that experience, I have felt an ongoing tender love for my colon. Instead of feeling fear, irritation or helplessness when it goes into distress of any kind, I now more readily respond to it by offering it my empowered love and gentleness.

I believe this shift in my relationship with my colon has probably been the most powerful treatment I've ever provided for it—inwardly or outwardly. I have also done this process since then with my brain when I've had a headache and with my stomach when it was feeling unsettled.

My experiences have highlighted the power of love when it comes to healing our bodies, an ingredient often missing in other methods of healing.

Shift in Attitude

As is evident in describing these experiences, I have noted another important change that has occurred around my body: a shift in my attitude and my relationship with it. During much of the earlier part of my life, I took my body for granted. Not only did I not value it much, I often felt it was my body that was responsible for keeping me from soaring as high spiritually as I wanted.

As a result, I didn't take very good care of my body. In fact, I neglected it in important ways and over-rode its symptoms of pain. And consequently, in my later years, I began encountering the results of my neglect. Chronic illnesses crept up on me, eventually compelling me to finally pay attention to my body and begin caring for it in a very conscious way.

I initially met the challenge of chronic illness with a lot of irritation and resentment that I directed toward my body, feeling it had "betrayed" me. My physical condition eventually became so debilitating, I couldn't even work anymore. Most of the time I was focused on the limitations my body was "imposing" on me. I have to smile now at that unenlightened response of irritation and resentment—I just didn't know any better.

I gradually began seeing how perfect it all was: finally focusing on my body was what was next on my path of learning—becoming aware that I was here with a physical body in order to learn how to awaken the self in which the body played an essential role. Leaving my body, either consciously or unconsciously, had always been an easy and natural thing for me to do. Now my challenge was to stay firmly within it.

Shift in Diet

Then, about three years ago, a strange thing happened. I was mulling over some difficulties I was having with my digestion. I knew I was eating all the "right" foods for a healthy diet. I was careful about sugar and starchy carbs, not eating dairy or wheat, avoiding processed foods, and eating organic whenever possible. And yet I was still having difficulty in digesting almost anything I was eating.

I became so confused and irritated about this at one point, I just demanded that my guides help me to know what my body needed. And I wanted to know *before* I ate something, rather than afterwards, so I could avoid it.

I didn't expect anything much to come from this irritated demand. But, much to my surprise, a few days later at the health food store, as I was pulling my usual foods off the shelves, I became aware of my stomach reacting to some of the things I was choosing. It was actually a feeling of my stomach turning over—a feeling of nausea.

I stopped and pondered this. Here were foods I'd eaten for a long time that I really loved and had believed to be good for me. And yet here also was this feeling of nausea. When I would put the item back on the shelf, the nausea would subside.

I suddenly realized my stomach was speaking to me about what it wanted. I went through the rest of the store paying attention to this sensation—and it continued. Some foods I'd simply look at (even when they were in packages or mixed with other foods), and my stomach would speak to me in this manner—nausea for a *No*, and a sense of lightness and desire for a *Yes*. I was amazed. Later, when I was simply thinking about particular foods, I would become aware of distinct messages about them from my stomach. It was extraordinary.

Somewhat to my dismay, however, I realized that many of my favorite foods were now on the No list. My list of possible foods and spices was greatly diminished. But now when I looked at foods and felt the nausea, I realized I really didn't want them anymore, anyway. It was all just habit and the memory of once having loved the foods that made me believe I wanted them.

Ever since that first experience, this communication with my stomach has continued. I have not only eaten many fewer varieties of foods—but less food, as well. I find I am eating because I am hungry, not because I look forward to eating for comfort or pleasure.

What I've discovered, however, is the diet that is appropriate for me is not a static one. There are times when my stomach occasionally expresses a desire for something that it's been rejecting for a long while. And yet, at the same time, I'm seeing that more and more foods and spices are being taken off my list. It seems to be getting increasingly limited as time goes on.

At one time I would have seen this as a sign that I was getting sicker and weaker with age. But I don't see it now that way at all. I see it as a sign of progression on my Ascension path. Our bodies are all shifting in a variety of ways; and for some of us, we can feel our bodies moving into a lighter state; heavy, dense, and spicy foods aren't working as well as before for this reason. On the higher levels in the Fifth Dimension, I imagine, food will probably not even be necessary.

But for now, as we progress through the Fourth Dimension, I think it is important for each of us to feel into our unique bodies and see what is appropriate now for us to eat. It's important to throw out all beliefs based on what experts have told us is "healthy" for us—and see what our particular bodies are saying about their unique needs at this point on our journey.

For some of us, animal protein is still important. For others, raw foods may need to be avoided. For still others, wheat or cow dairy may actually be okay. It's really important to be in touch with what our bodies are telling us, and to keep in constant communication with them as we move closer and closer to shifting into our light bodies.

Beliefs about Aging

Another shift I've become aware of during the last few years revolves around beliefs I have about my body as it gets older. Like many people in their elder years, I was holding the collective belief that as my age increased, my body would show classic signs of aging and become less functional. I assumed I would naturally get aches and pains, and certain organs would probably begin to work less effectively.

Of course, those are the beliefs that have come from living in the Third Dimension for thousands of years, from experiencing the reality of aging and death over and over again in that reality structure. I believed that the body could only get so old, and then it would die.

Then at one point I remembered hearing that in the Ascension process we would at some point begin getting younger and healthier as our third-dimensional bodies began morphing into fifth-dimensional bodies. Whenever I heard this, I always accepted it as a probable truth. But it was never clear to me that it might happen for ME.

Because my body was getting old and also had been ill in numerous ways, I assumed I'd probably be someone who would have to leave my current body—and simply create a new one in the Fifth Dimension. (There are confusing reports on what will actually happen at the point of transition, although certain teachings say we will have the choice to either keep our current body or create a new one.) At any rate, my body just seemed too worn out and dense to be one that could easily heal itself and turn into light.

A Startling Reverse-Aging Experience

Well, last year I had an experience that really put that assumption into question. A strange and uncomfortable thing began happening to me: heart palpitations and a very rapid pulse.

One morning my pulse climbed to 135 and my heart was jumping out of my chest. Panicked, I called my doctor and, after hearing just a few words about my pulse, she told me to get off the phone and call an ambulance immediately. I knew she thought I might be having a heart attack, so I did as she directed. I called 911.

After spending five hours in the ER taking tests, x-rays and scans, the doctor finally came in to tell me my heart was fine—nothing wrong with it. The only thing that could be causing my symptoms was that I had too much thyroid in my system.

I told her that couldn't be true, that ever since childhood I'd always had a low thyroid condition. In fact, at a certain point I had been put on massive doses of thyroid medication—which did some good, but never entirely relieved the low thyroid symptoms. Doctors always puzzled over my body's slow absorption of thyroid in any form I'd take it. So I knew she had to be wrong.

She looked skeptical when I told her all this. But I was adamant; I knew my body and all I'd been through in dealing with my thyroid. She concluded that they'd take a blood test and send the results to my regular doctor and then released me.

My Stubborn Belief System

A few days later I saw my regular doctor. She had looked at the results of the test and told me I had way too much thyroid in my blood and that I needed immediately to cut the dosage in half. I panicked, hearing this, remembering the terrible symptoms I'd dealt with in the past when I'd tried reducing the amount of thyroid medication I was taking. I was certain that there was no way, after a lifetime of having to treat a low thyroid condition, that I could have too much thyroid in my body.

But I was desperate, so I knew I had to give it a try. I took half my usual dosage the next day. Almost immediately my pulse slowed down some. I was amazed. After all these years, could my low-producing thyroid suddenly be producing more thyroid? Could it actually be getting healthy at this point? It didn't seem possible.

Another week passed and I saw that my pulse was again increasing. At that point, I started thinking maybe a miracle actually was happening. Maybe my body was beginning to turn itself around; perhaps it was starting to become a younger, healthier body, after all.

I took a chance and again cut my dosage of thyroid medication in half. And it worked! I was now on a very miniscule amount of thyroid and I was feeling fine. My pulse returned to normal. And since then I have stopped taking any medication at all. It seems that, out of the blue, my thyroid healed itself.

An Indication of What's to Come?

Is this a sign of what we have to look forward to? Will our bodies, as they continue to turn to a crystalline form, automatically begin to heal? It seems likely this could happen.

It seems plausible to me that this physical crisis I experienced was a gift given to me to begin shifting my belief system around what's possible for my body at this point—and what might be possible for all our bodies as we continue to move into higher consciousness.

In any case, although it was a difficult life passage to discover the miracle, I am immensely grateful for it. After so radically reducing the thyroid medication I was taking, I also decided to stop using the hormone creams I had been on for many years, as well as another medication I thought I could never get off of. And I have actually felt better than I have in a long, long time.

Aging, Ascension, and "Youthening"

It can get confusing at times to try to figure out what exactly is happening in our bodies. There are four different things that might be going on when we're not feeling well: an illness, an aging symptom, a temporary Ascension symptom, and a "youthening" experience as I've described above. They can all be very similar.

It's not easy to decide what to do in these situations. If we're working with doctors or health practitioners who don't have a clue about Ascension or its implications on the physical body, it can be difficult to explain these things to them. I find that when I can, I just ride the symptom out, alert to its possibly getting worse. If it disappears after a while, I take it as a sign that it's an Ascension symptom. If it doesn't, I look for help.

Even if it is an Ascension symptom, if it's too uncomfortable to be living with it, I know I can find help by taking herbs or other supplements and sometimes simply Tylenol for pain. Acupuncture, massage, chiropractic and physical therapy can also be helpful. It doesn't matter whether a physical ailment is a symptom of aging, illness, an Ascension symptom or a sign of youthening. If there's pain or illness, we do usually need to attend to it in some way.

But it can be helpful to not automatically believe ourselves to be suffering from aging or falling ill when we don't feel well. Knowing that something could possibly be an Ascension symptom or even a sign of youthening can create a feeling of optimism and less worry—an attitude that always assists a body to heal.

Creating a Higher Dimensional Perspective

One thing I know is that now that we're traveling through the Fourth Dimension, in certain ways everything is actually becoming easier. For many of us manifestation seems to be happening more quickly, it's easier to move out of negativity, easier to feel joy, easier to experience deep love.

Even though many of us may also be experiencing some challenging things as old patterns of limitation and wounding are arising to be released, we are also experiencing more spontaneous openings of joy and love for no reason at all. At times a new feeling of freedom just sings through us, a delicious lightness of being. So why wouldn't our bodies be healing as well?

Of course I am not qualified to give medical advice, and none of what I'm saying should be construed as that. If there is any concern that actual illness may be occurring, naturally it's important to see a health practitioner about it.

But I do encourage people I work with to reflect on what is happening inside themselves—both in their emotional lives and in their bodies—to observe if healing is indeed happening. Have certain psychological patterns that used to occur regularly in their lives begun to decrease or disappear? Have certain life-long symptoms in their bodies ceased recently?

It's important that we become aware of a third-dimensional belief that bodies can't spontaneously heal. And that bodies are always open to disease and will eventually get old and then die.

All this was true in the Third Dimension. But we have moved out of that dimension now. The only thing that can make it look like we haven't is our habitual limited beliefs and expectations about our lives. If we can shift our perspective to a more open, trusting one of expecting miracles—who knows what can occur?

Chapter 6

Shifting Relationships

Perhaps the area of life in which I've noticed the most change happening in people's lives is that of relationships. This makes sense, as relationships seem to be both the most fulfilling and the most challenging area of life for many people.

It's also to be expected, as there's a phenomenon that appears to be happening for many of us: a drifting away from certain family members and old friends who have been in our lives for a long time.

Dissolution of Karmic Bonds

Many of us in the Ascension process are beginning to see that, as our vibration rises, we feel less and less connected to certain people we grew up with and felt a connection to during much of our lives. What I'm hearing from my guides is this is because many of our karmic bonds are dissolving at this time. Karma with our families and other important people in our lives is ending.

It can feel strange to no longer feel the attachment to certain people that had always been there. We can feel alone and disconnected as our usual engagement with them begins to dissipate. It's important to understand that this is a natural occurrence in the Ascension process. As our karmic bonds to our family and friends loosen and dissolve—and also as our vibration rises—we can expect that we may no longer feel all that comfortable around some of them, especially if they're remaining at a lower vibration.

In particular, when we're with people who go on and on about their pain, guilt, and resentment, it can get uncomfortably boring to listen to them. Indeed, it can actually become painful—especially if we try to get them to see a more positive, optimistic picture of themselves or situations they're in and they can't hear us. As time goes on, we can probably expect this to happen more and more with certain family members. At some point we may find we really don't wish to spend much time with them anymore.

I find that a sensitivity to vibrational differences can get increasingly uncomfortable over time. During these times when our vibrations are lifting so rapidly, our nervous systems can become extra sensitive and vulnerable. Because of this, we need to take care of ourselves and not put ourselves in situations that aggravate us or cause us undue stress.

It can be painful to feel yourself wanting to detach from family members or old friends you love. You may feel their hurt or confusion. But it's important to follow your intuition on this and take care of yourself by limiting the time you spend with them.

However, this desire to pull away from them need not affect the level of love you hold for them. In fact, you might realize that your love for them is actually greater than ever, that you're moving into a true experience of unconditional love with them. You just don't need to be around them a lot to feel this.

Looking at Our Old 3D Relationship Patterns

Learning how to deal with the experience of loosening karmic bonds is just one relationship challenge many of us are facing at this point in our Ascension process. There is another challenge that many of us are also experiencing: a need to look at how we have functioned in relationship in general throughout our lives—and the kind of suffering we have caused both ourselves and others through our unconscious dysfunctional patterns.

Most of these patterns that cause us disappointment, grief, anger and hurt in relationships are ones we took on naturally growing up in a third-dimensional world in which people were spiritually asleep and unaware of what authentic love that exists in higher dimensions might look like.

The patterns include certain dynamics that form patterns that are generally called "co-dependent" by mental health practitioners. Labels such as "caretaking", "enabling" are often given to one of the partners in such a relationship; and "narcissistic" or "abusive" are often given to the other. The dynamics in such a relationship are of course viewed as "dysfunctional" and "unhealthy."

If we are currently involved in relationships at this point that might be labeled in this way, we are likely finding there's a new intensity that has arisen in them lately. The fifth-dimensional energies that are entering our relationship dynamics are intensifying painful emotions we may have been able to ignore until now, but no longer. Often they bring up unresolved issues from all the way back to childhood. This process can be extremely painful.

3D Dependence in Relationships

It's easy enough to identify relationship patterns we have that we've always known to be somewhat dysfunctional. There are certainly plenty of books and webinars out there that can help us find solutions to how to shift our patterns into healthier ones. And these patterns, naturally, are ones we need to tend to as we ascend into higher vibrations, or we're going to get really uncomfortable.

However, from a fifth-dimensional point of view, there is one reason typical mainstream relationship experts rarely if ever raise that in many ways has been the cause of *all* relationship difficulties. And that is the common 3D belief that the purpose of relationships with family, spouses, and good friends is to give us the essential sense that we are lovable, valuable, and important.

In the old third-dimensional paradigm we all grew up in, we were taught that our loved ones were there to fulfill this emotional need. This belief sounds so right—and warm and cozy, in a way. It's what we've always accepted to be true. And to some degree, we have all managed to survive certain situations because we have felt our emotional needs to be at least mostly met by our relationships.

But as we move forward on our Ascension path, it is valuable to question this belief. Is that really the purpose of relationship? If you think about it, you can see how this assumption includes a belief that we are not inherently whole and able to see and experience our own value, lovableness, and inherent worth, without someone else's help.

And more importantly, it means that we must continue to put up with all the grief and anger we can sometimes feel when our loved-ones don't give us what we feel they "should" give us on the emotional level.

How many conflicts throughout our lives has this tacit agreed-upon arrangement—that our loved-ones are there to fill our emotional needs—created for us? How many times have the people we've assigned the task of meeting these needs fallen short in fulfilling them? And how many times have we fallen short in taking care of their emotional needs? So many power struggles steeped in feelings of hurt, betrayal and guilt arise out of this usually unconscious agreement between people that their relationships exist in order to fill each other's emotional needs.

When we look at this issue, we can see how it points back to our need, as we shift into fifth-dimensional consciousness, to truly develop a sense of love for ourselves and to be able to rely on *that*, first and foremost, for our sense of feeling valuable, loved and respected. We need to see that if we are truly going to get free of hurt and blame and anger in our relationships, it is not the job of other people to give us a sense of emotional wholeness; it is up to us.

The Freedom in 5D Relationships

If we're used to having relationships based on the typical 3D model, it may sound as if a relationship without this agreement to take responsibility for each other's needs would be a dry, unemotional and disconnected type of relationship. But until we experience one in which this is not the agreement, we can't know this.

When we move into fifth-dimensional consciousness, we can find that without these types of emotional demands on each other, we can have warm, loving, and highly-fulfilling relationships that run smoothly without a lot of drama. We can discover that although we do give each other a great deal of love, respect and support, we are not dependent on each other's love to feel good about ourselves, to feel valuable and important.

The love we receive from others is a bonus, an overflow that is much appreciated and valued; but is not *needed* at the core of our being, because we are able to provide the love we need from within ourselves. There is therefore no emotional demand that the others we're in relationship with give us the love we need to feel good about ourselves.

And, very importantly, our love for them springs solely from our true caring and compassion for them—not from a need or a demand within us that they provide us with something in return. It's an unconditional love, free of demands that a person act in a certain way or be something different from who they are.

Of course, this idealized version of a relationship may sound unattainable at this point. And it probably is for most of us still shrugging off our 3D habit patterns and beliefs. But it can be seen as a goal, one that will one day be achievable as we lift our vibration toward fifth-dimensional consciousness.

The most important focus for us to be able to experience and express this kind of love for others is to learn how to love ourselves in that way first. I speak at greater length about the process of learning how to fully love ourselves in Chapter 8. The task of learning self-love is at the core of all our Ascension learning. Being cut off from the true knowing of ourselves as spiritual Beings, as we were for so long in the Third Dimension, has made it next to impossible to know our true inherent lovableness and value.

But thankfully, our journey back into full consciousness is awakening us once again to the incredible magnificence of who we are and how we truly don't need any outer reinforcement or reflection to let us know and experience our inherent value and beauty. It is self-evident. And, among other things, this realization can make our relationships with others much more fulfilling and flow with greater ease and joy.

Meanwhile, as we find our way through this shift of awareness and experience in our relationships, it's very important to find and to rest in compassion for ourselves. This is not an easy transition to make.

We are emerging out of thousands of years of awkward, unawakened attempts to find love and safety from our relationships with other people who themselves have not been awake or fulfilled. There are a lot of age-old beliefs and illusions we need to have the courage to shed in order to discover how truly free and awake relationships can be.

Shifting Primary Relationships

With all this going on, a particularly challenging relationship to maintain during this period of Ascension can be one with a primary partner. Part of this is due to the fact that, even without the factor of Ascension involved, whenever there is significant spiritual or psychological growth happening for one or both partners, the strength of the relationship always seems to be tested.

This is because there's a specific energetic "match" that has to be maintained for a primary relationship to work smoothly. Often this is a match in the level of self-worth and self-love each person feels. And when one or both partners begin shifting emotionally or spiritually in an important way, the match can begin to wobble.

But with the Ascension process also pushing people into change in such a rapid fashion, those in a primary relationship often find themselves shifting dramatically in how they're relating to each other. And this can cause a rocky mismatch in the relationship, at least for a while.

If couples can understand this and give each other space to move through their own changes with as much freedom as possible, there can be hope of moving through the shifting more comfortably. Certain couples are discovering, however, that with the inner shifts they're experiencing, their partnership is no longer working for them at this point. It's time to split up and move in different directions.

Yet whether couples stay together or not, there seems to be an interesting phenomenon happening with a number of them: either way, partners are finding during these times they are experiencing a deeper love for their partner than they've ever known before—even with those partners they may be choosing to leave.

Clearing of Past Relationships

This deepening of love can also happen in some cases for those who are no longer together with a particular partner, even if they haven't seen that person for years.

I know a woman who had left an unhappy marriage a number of years before and had attempted to move on in her life. But since she had never had true closure with her husband, she had not been able to let him go. Nor had she been able to let go of nagging feelings of disempowerment, resentment and grief she'd experienced in the relationship.

There came a point when she finally realized she needed to meet with him and speak her truth to him—something she'd never had the courage to do before. She was frightened of meeting with him, fearing she would repeat the same patterns with him she had before. But finally she decided to do it anyway.

Much to her surprise, she was able to easily stand in her power and speak to him from a calm and centered place. Her detachment and inner strength surprised her. She had not realized how much she had grown—and how relatively easy it was for her to do this.

And, very importantly, she found she was experiencing a great deal of love for him—just as he was. She still saw what she experienced as narcissism in him and a lack of true understanding of who she was, but it didn't matter. She was feeling a love for him that extended far beyond what she'd ever been able to feel or express during her marriage.

It was a love that transcended this life, one that emanated from a higher aspect of herself that she identified as the Soul—profound and unconditional. And yet she knew it was no longer right for them to be together. They had completed what they'd come into this life to experience together. She was immensely grateful for this experience. It finally freed her to let go of him and begin moving forward in her life.

I myself had a similar experience to this, although mine happened in the sleep state one night. I was with my ex-husband, whom I hadn't seen for years. I had been aware of a deep love I knew I still had for him; I had always felt this, no matter what had transpired between us. But in this very lucid experience, he and I were totally immersed in a powerful love I had never before felt.

It was not only the depth of the love that was different—it was the quality of it. The love was so profound, so old, so familiar, and it had a transcendent aspect to it. We were just looking at each other, enveloped in the field of this love, and there was nothing else present but this love.

I was aware in the experience that this was who we actually were—two Souls with immense love for each other. I knew we had known each other forever and had lived many, many lifetimes together. This time around we had agreed to come back with the intention to finally balance all karma with each other, so that only love would be present. And I knew we had achieved this.

What was surprising to me was that there was absolutely no sadness or regret that we were no longer together in our physical lives. I knew it was all as it should be; how it had all unfolded was what was right for us. Our separation didn't in any way affect the love we had for each other.

I woke up in a state of bliss. I knew I had been given a great gift—the memory of being with a Soul I deeply loved and the experience of our love for each other at this higher vibrational level. It moves me still to simply remember this experience.

I believe that we probably all have these kinds of love-infused experiences in the higher realms of light in the sleep state and that we simply don't remember them. But as time goes on and we near the Fifth Dimension in our spiritual evolution, I believe we may be bringing back the memory of them more and more often.

I also sense we can begin having these higher-love experiences more in our everyday waking lives, as well. It seems we are not ascending into the Fifth Dimension—it's actually descending down into us where we now are in our lives.

Shifting Relationships with our Parents

For most people, the relationship with their parents tends to be the relationship most fraught with unresolved emotional issues. It's often that relationship which, if left unresolved, will serve to hold us back in third-dimensional consciousness.

As we get older we can come to understand that our parents were naturally flawed human beings who did their best to be parents to us despite all the personal issues with which they were themselves dealing. And yet it is often still difficult to let go of deep-seated feelings of anger, abandonment, hurt, and betrayal we felt toward them as children. So much of what doesn't work well in our lives seems to stem back to our painful childhood experiences.

Childhood "Stuff" Doesn't Always Start in Childhood

Although this is usually true, I've found in the past-life work I've done with people over the years that it's important to realize that the really important dysfunctional patterns that appeared to come about in our childhood years with our parents are actually patterns we brought in with us from other lifetimes. They didn't begin with our parents.

Our childhood with them was simply the first "setting" we came up with in our Soul plan for us to begin working on the karmic patterns in this lifetime. We chose our parents very carefully, knowing they would be able to set up the circumstances necessary to give us the opportunity we needed to balance the patterns we came in with.

If we look at our lives once we left childhood, we can usually see that people in other important relationships—especially our romantic partners and our children—have played similar roles for us that our parents played. They may seem at first glance to be very different from our parents. But when we look more deeply, we can see that the way we are triggered by them is often very similar to how we were triggered by our parents while growing up.

In fact, these relationships in which we play out familiar dysfunctional roles have been brought forward time and again in our lives, giving us multiple opportunities to play them out—until hopefully, at last we learn to let them go. Employers, friends, and colleagues have also stepped in, usually unknowingly, to perform this service for us.

When we can see the bigger picture in this way, it makes it a lot easier to see our parents for who they are: Souls we likely have great love for, beloveds who agreed to come in and play out pivotal roles in our lives in hopes of helping us free ourselves through our relationships with them. We have probably incarnated with them countless times before and played out roles as their parents, spouses or siblings.

Therefore, what seems important is to not focus on our parents and what they "did" or "didn't do" to us—but rather to see what patterns, emotions and beliefs we experienced with them, and take ownership of them. These are what we created at one time and brought with us into this lifetime with hopes of finally completing them.

Many of us have spent decades of working through issues with our parents, and have found some relief and clarity about them. I, for one, did a lot of this kind of personal work in my earlier years, using all the various forms of therapy and healing, both traditional and alternative, that have been available since the 1960s.

And at some point I felt I had finally come to total forgiveness and an experience of detachment with my mother, father, and stepfather—all of whom have since died. At some point, whenever I happened to think of them, I usually experienced a calm love for each of them, along with a sense of peace and wishing them well wherever they now might be.

An Extraordinary Healing Experience

In fact I had a very impactful experience with all three of them during a process I did while attending the Oneness University in India back in 2006, learning how to give the Oneness Blessing (or *deeksha*). In a room with about 200 people during a 21-day intensive course, the lights went down and we were instructed to close our eyes and simply begin thinking about our parents and see what would happen.

It was always amazing to me what would transpire in that room when just simple instructions like that would be given. Almost immediately I began hearing weeping around me—moans, whimpering, and deep sobbing.

Surprisingly, my experience was a little different. As soon as I closed my eyes, an amazing scenario began to unfold. I clearly saw in my mind's eye a woman somewhere in her thirties walk out on a type of lighted "platform" in front of me and peer into the darkened room, as if she were looking for someone. Suddenly she spotted me; and I realized with a start that it was my mother.

But this was a woman I'd never really known, because she now looked younger than she'd been when she'd given birth to me. And much to my surprise and delight, she looked happy and carefree. My heart filled with love, as I realized I'd probably never, ever seen her like this when she was alive. I remembered her as a deeply unhappy woman for most of her life.

She came over to me and we hugged in a way we had never been able to in our life here together—with a deep and clear love for each other. As I gazed into her eyes, I could see her profound caring for me. After the extremely difficult relationship we had shared in this lifetime, it was amazing to experience her like this. We sat down and began catching up like old friends united after a long time apart.

At one point we both glanced toward the "platform" she'd first appeared on, and there was a man somewhere in his thirties who was peering into the room where we stood. He looked confused and was conferring with a man next to him who was pointing toward us and explaining something to him. My mother suddenly exclaimed, "That's your father!" With joy, she called him over.

I was amazed. I didn't recognize this man at all. He looked very different from the man I'd known for the first five years of my life before he left us. He looked young and as yet unburdened by life. And he also looked kind of clueless.

With some prompting, he finally came over and first embraced my mother and then me. I realized suddenly that I knew him, really knew him, and had a great deal of love for him. This was an emotion I had never felt for him as a child, because I didn't really know him. He was never home much during the five years he and my mother were still together after my birth; and when he was, he always seemed to be drunk and angry with my mother. They often fought viciously with each other, and I tended to stay out of his way as much as possible. But here he was now, and I knew there was a deep Soul-love we held for each other. What a discovery!

A few moments later, to my surprise, a third figure appeared on the "platform"—and this one I recognized: it was my step-father. He immediately saw us and came and embraced my mother and me—and then my mother introduced him to my father. I had to laugh at how this scene was playing out—my father and stepfather actually speaking together like friends, with my mother talking animatedly with both of them—nothing that would ever have happened when they were all alive.

Although I had had some serious karmic interactions with my stepfather when he was alive, which I have had to live with ever since, everything now seemed clear between us. There was just a deep love and appreciation for each other.

This whole scenario happened within about a fifteen-minute period—all of it extremely clear and real. And then it was apparently time for them to go. They all turned to me with deep appreciation—thanking me for the opportunity I'd provided them to finally meet and experience a profound healing with all of us together. And then they turned and disappeared. As can be imagined, this experience deeply impacted me and I felt a profound gratitude for having had it.

Help of the Increasing Ascension Energies

With my own experience and in hearing others speak of powerful healing interactions they also are having with their parents—either alive in person or in an altered state with parents who have passed on—I do believe the releasing of old dysfunctional patterns is getting easier and easier. I'm beginning to trust that we simply have to set our intention to be free of these patterns and be willing to accept whatever comes forward in our lives to help us do this, and patterns will begin to clear in a rapid fashion. Ascension is providing this opportunity.

I have a student who demonstrated this really well to me. She had been living a very responsible and successful life as an adult for a number of years when, after a series of strange and unfortunate events in her life, she found she needed to go live with her father again for a while, as she had nowhere else to go.

Life had stripped her of all ability to take care of herself financially; and to her shame and consternation, she found herself back living with him (and his new wife she'd never gotten along with), dependent on him in a number of different ways.

It became evident that this was a time for her to let go of all illusions about who she thought she was and what she was to accomplish in the world. It was also a time to finally face unresolved issues with her father. The number of months she felt stuck there in that situation compelled her to finally move through patterns she'd likely lived with many lifetimes and had not been able to resolve.

I was struck over and over again by her immense courage to take responsibility for her own stuff with her father. I could see that the Ascension process had her by the throat. But she realized that her clear intention for final freedom from her childhood patterns had brought this situation in to help her—and it wouldn't let her go until she got what she needed to learn. Although it was difficult, in understanding what was happening, she just kept moving through one challenging situation after another.

I could also see the new fourth and fifth-dimensional energies flowing through her, as it became easier and easier as time went on to move with surprising speed through anger, depression, and grief. The energies were like a wind blowing through her, cleansing her. And then there came a time when it was apparent that she was complete with the process; she was finally free to leave.

To her delight, she found she was experiencing a profound and clear love she'd never had before for her father. He likely had no awareness of the bigger picture that was occurring for both of them. But he must have reaped the benefits of the enormous love she grew into, both for herself and for him.

I know that these freeing energies are now here for all of us to take advantage of in clearing old dysfunctional patterns that are not in alignment with our emerging fifth-dimensional selves. Traditional therapy techniques and time-consuming healing processes may no longer be necessary.

I believe that as time passes, it will become easier and easier for us to release deep-seated patterns we've carried with us throughout countless lifetimes in the Third Dimension, without a lot of intense probing and releasing.

In some cases, there can even be miracles. We don't have to work as hard to clear stuff as we once did. We simply need to bring awareness to the patterns when they arise so we may consciously release them. And we can discover that enormous assistance is now present for doing this.

I was speaking the other day to a friend of mine who gives counseling to a number of women. She mentioned that many of these women have never had any kind of counseling before, nor have they ever done much introspection. And yet they seem to be having awakening experiences and deep realizations about themselves that she herself began having only after years of spiritual growth work.

Part of the reason for this is probably that there are those of us who have been on a path of awakening for years and have helped to "clear the way" for those coming behind us to awaken more quickly. But I also believe we're in different times now, and the light that is pouring onto the Earth in these times of Ascension is also making it easier for everyone to move more quickly along their awakening path.

Shifting Relationships with Our Children

Many of us who are parents believe that our love for our children is a love like no other love we can feel. It may be that something exists about the particular biological connection when we have given our DNA to another Soul so they can incarnate in a physical body.

And of course, just like with our own parents, spouses, partners and good friends, there is likely a deep love on a Soul level that exists between us—or we wouldn't have decided before incarnating to provide the physical vehicle for our children.

But for this same reason, we also probably have unfinished karmic issues we've agreed to work on together in this lifetime as parent and child. And this can make our experience as parents difficult at times—especially now that we and our children are both also meeting challenges in our personal Ascension processes.

Children Have their own Life Paths

It may seem counter-intuitive, but many of us with children are discovering that our Ascension process is actually pulling us away from our children. We are feeling less attached or even connected to them. The personal love we may have had with them, with all its needs, demands and enmeshment, is transforming into a love that is less entwined and more neutral.

This can sound like a healthy transformation (and it is), but it can be distressing for parents who have been very attached to their children and greatly involved in their lives until now. If they've experienced a sense of being needed and loved from their children, as well as a sense of belonging, a feeling of abandonment might arise.

Another unsettling thing that can happen is when our children go off in a direction that seems very different from how we've always imagined and believed they should—and there seems to be nothing we can do about it. No matter how connected we may still feel to them as they grow up and how responsible we may still feel for them in their lives, we really can do very little at times to protect them from their pain and the mistakes we may believe they are making. All we can do is stand by and continue to love them without conditions.

What we need to remember is that our children are separate human beings with their own paths in life and their own karma to resolve, something we can do nothing about. They have their own Soul contracts and plans they are following—much of which, especially in their later years, has nothing at all to do with us. And now, with Ascension happening, their paths may be very different from what even they had imagined.

Like many parents I know, I went through a sometimes excruciating period in my daughter's development into an adult when she decided (consciously or unconsciously) to move into the natural and healthy period of individuation and separation from me. Unlike many children who experience this in their early and mid-adolescence, it began for her in her late teens and continued into her twenties.

It was especially painful for me because she and I had been so close and intimate up until that time. It was often noted by others around us how "wonderful" a relationship we had. Our love and intimate knowing of each other was very evident.

I had felt fortunate that I didn't have to go through what so many parents go through during their children's adolescence. My daughter and I could always talk things through; we could always very easily understand each other's point of view. We very seldom had clashes.

So when this breakaway period did finally happen—and it was severe—it was especially difficult for me. In fact, for almost ten years I felt that I had simply "lost" her. It was as if something had just been ripped from my heart. She was so precious to me, so important—that if I hadn't had some understanding of what was likely going on due to Ascension, I don't know if I could have made it through those painful years.

We finally did make it through this rough period in our relationship and are out the other end of it. But our relationship has dramatically morphed into one in which we are now simply warm and deeply caring friends. The parent-child relationship seems essentially to be gone.

It took a while for me to adjust to this. But it really became clear to me that she definitely had a plan before birth to take an entirely different path in life than I could ever have imagined or wished for her. And once I accepted that—and truly understood that she is a very separate individual from me, no matter how connected I feel to her—we could now have a relationship that is deeply satisfying for both of us.

It is interesting to me that a number of parents I know with grown children are undergoing especially difficult times with their children—much more so than ever before in my counseling career over the years. Ascension seems to be demanding that we focus on consciously clearing all karmic patterns with our children as quickly as possible—or very painful relationships with them may develop.

Knowing Our Children from Before

One thing that can help is understanding that our relationship with our children today is simply a current relationship we have with them; we have likely known them in numerous other lifetimes—and perhaps even before we first incarnated on the Earth.

A few years ago I had an extraordinary experience on the inner planes that explained a lot to me about my deep connection with my daughter. I was in a workshop with Christine Day, a woman who describes herself as a "Pleiadian Ambassador", and was deep in a meditation process she was leading.

During this workshop I had been waking up very clearly to the fact of my own Pleiadian heritage, something that was both surprising and extremely impactful for me. Ancient memories were flooding in, along with profound feelings and openings in my mind to other realms of knowing and experience.

At one point the realization suddenly came to me that my daughter was an old, old beloved friend of mine from the Pleiades. With this realization came a torrent of tears infused with a love that far surpassed the deep love I already knew I had for her.

Just remembering this experience can immediately drop me into the space in which love fills me to overflowing within moments. It's one of those experiences that actually feels almost like a blow to the heart. It stuns me, stops me in my tracks and I plummet into a depth of delicious love. But initially it can almost be painful, as the shift from my everyday consciousness can sometimes be abrupt and dramatic.

My guess is that many of us who are beginning to remember where we came from before we began incarnating on the Earth may have these kinds of connections with our children (and grandchildren). Even just intuiting this to be true, without knowing particulars, can assist us to release our children more cleanly from old parental patterns and move into a whole new relationship with them infused with more love, respect and understanding.

Fear of Leaving our Children Behind

The Ascension process many of us are experiencing has even further complicated the relationships certain parents have with their children. I have heard them express a fear that if they are choosing to ascend during this lifetime and their children are not making that same choice, they may have to leave their children "behind".

This is a very understandable and poignant concern. Especially if the children are still young at this point and dependent on their parents, of course the fear will come up about who will take care of them if their parents are moving on to a higher dimension.

My understanding about this issue is this: If you are a parent of young, dependent children—have no fear. You will be with them until they can be on their own. You have contracts with them that will ensure this. You will simply be operating eventually from within a fifth-dimensional consciousness—and lucky them for this! But you will still be here with them.

AND—if you're like many parents on the path of Ascension these days, it's likely your young children are too. In fact, if you're really aware, you'll probably find that you can learn a whole lot from your children about fifth-dimensional consciousness. They may be waiting for *you* to catch up.

If your children are older and on their own, and you have these fears of moving on without them, it's a different story. Some of our adult children may be among those on the Earth at this time who are choosing to continue on in other places in the universe where third-dimensional lives are still being lived. And you may feel yourself drifting from them in certain ways at this point.

The important thing to remember is that although you're not feeling connected to them as you have in the past because your karmic ties are loosening, you can still stay connected to them at the heart level. Your heart will never forget them. And indeed, as Souls, you will always stay connected through your love.

Highly-Evolved Children Coming In

There are parents with very young children being born today, especially since 2012, who are facing unusually unique situations with their children. Many of these new children are what have been called "crystal children" or "light children"—Souls with very little or no karma coming onto the planet at this time to eventually lead us all fully into the Golden Age.

These children are wise, highly evolved beings who often understand much more about life and spiritual realities than their parents and grandparents, and it takes a very conscious and careful approach to parenting to guide them well to where they can reach their highest potential.

Parents with these children are indeed fortunate—what a blessing and honor to give birth to such beings! But it can also be challenging to have to learn ways of parenting quite different from what they may have learned from their own parents. Listening very carefully to their children, both inwardly and outwardly, is essential, as these children know well what they need from their parents. And they will often let their parents know in no uncertain terms when they are not receiving it.

Many of these children are also ultra-sensitive, not only to certain foods and substances, but also to energies. They often tend to be extremely empathic and easily absorb any inharmonious energies that are emitted around them. So parents need to be very aware of this and to keep their own emotions on as even a keel as they can when they're around their children.

Relating Soul-to-Soul

No matter how you may find yourself relating to all your family members and old friends these days, something you may realize is that you are relating to them—even if you're feeling more distance from them lately—on a whole different level. With greater detachment from your old karmic patterns, you can now more clearly see them as Souls who are finding their way through these confusing times, just as you are. And you can explore relating to them on this level—Soul-to-Soul.

It can be very freeing to do this. You can still be aware of all their usual personality characteristics, some of which may be irritating to you; but your need for them to be any different from how they are has disappeared. And as you relate to them from this level, you can watch as they too may rise up to match you on that level where Souls come together very naturally in love—even if there is little left to hold you together in your physical life.

When Karma is Complete

In working with dozens of people in the last year or so, I have seen a trend of what looks like karma completing itself more and more in people's lives. It's very exciting.

With this karmic completion, there's a sense with these people that they've reached a point of "pause" in their lives. Much of what they came into this life to balance and complete has been accomplished, and they're now ready to move into what might be next in their lives.

This is very interesting to me, as it appears to be an indication that people are indeed moving forward at a rapid rate in leaving their third-dimensional lives behind. And, for many, it means they're ready to begin their spiritual purpose.

If you think about it, this may be happening in your life. Karma may be completing itself in different areas of your life. Or it may be coming to a "climax"—like a final test before it's finished. If this is the case, it can be freeing just to realize this is what's happening; it can give you the encouragement to keep moving forward in meeting whatever is unfolding to complete it, once and for all.

At the same time be aware that when the karma is finished, it can initially leave you feeling somewhat "untethered" for a while. Even if it's been uncomfortable or painful to be tied to someone or to a group of people by karmic bonds for a long time, it can feel strange and ungrounded to no longer feel those bonds holding you in a familiar place. You no longer know where you "belong." You've moved into an unknown space of reality.

But you'll see, with a little trust and patience, that a new direction and a new sense of belonging will develop in due time, without the old sense of being bound to people around you. And, with this, you'll be much freer to navigate in a direction that feels fulfilling to you and to create relationships that are authentically nurturing, creative and fulfilling.

Soul Families Gathering

Often what starts to happen for many at this point on their Ascension path is that new people begin coming into their lives, people who are operating at a level of frequency similar to their own. There's an instantaneous comfort and recognition in meeting these new people and often a sense that they'll be working together in some way. A Soul connection is recognized and there's a feeling that they've known these new people before. It's a feeling that their Soul family is gathering.

For others, this meeting of new people hasn't begun yet, and they're feeling alone, except for occasional conversations online they may have with others like themselves. My sense is that those who are feeling alone will not stay alone for long. Soul communities are gathering; many are finding people they have contracts with around their spiritual missions.

But if you're one of those who is still waiting for this to happen, know that it's just a matter of having patience and waiting for Divine timing. Trust that you're not going to be alone forever in your desire to assist humanity and the Earth through the Ascension process. Others will come along to join you at some point.

Meanwhile, move through whatever relationship issues that may be arising for you with the people who are currently around you. See if you can successfully complete any relationships that are not nurturing to you, and make more room inside yourself for those that are.

Chapter 7

New Relationships with Spiritual Teachers

Many of us who have been on a conscious path of awakening for any length of time have spent time along the way with certain spiritual teachers with whom we've felt a resonance. I believe teachers can be really helpful for us most of the time, so long as they have a certain amount of psychological maturity and awareness, as well as spiritual awareness.

And if by chance they don't and act in unconscious or hurtful ways toward their students, they at least offer an opportunity for people to work through any unresolved authority-parent issues they may still have.

Living in these times of spiritual transformation, however, it seems increasingly clear that teacher-student relationships are shifting, just as our other relationships are. I've heard it said that this age we're moving into is about giving up both the student and the teacher roles we may be playing and realizing we're really all in this together. It certainly seems that the time of giving one's power over to a guru or teacher is on its way out. Everyone is waking up, and it's mainly through inner guidance that continued awakening will take place.

This doesn't mean that we should give up all work we're doing with teachers. There are always people further along on the path who can give us guidance and help point the way. What needs to shift is our relationship to them if we are giving them any power over our lives or if we are listening to them rather than to our deeper selves to tell us what is right for us.

Some of us have had struggles with the teachers we've chosen. In my case, I know that in part I was working out unresolved issues with my mother in my relationships with certain teachers I've had. But part of it was also due to a knowing that the spiritual teacher-student relationship for me was already shifting, even as far back as the 1970s—and that I didn't want to get caught in old, dependent relationships with them.

Teachers Who "Fall"

I studied with a particular teacher back then who in his younger days was both very powerful in his spiritual awareness and clear in his energy. Unfortunately, at some point he seemed to fall into the typical ego traps so many spiritual teachers fall into: those of money, sex, and power. These traps can be subtle and hidden, and a surprising number of teachers seem to be blinded by them.

It can be heart-breaking, because many of them also bring forward important and transformative teachings. And it can be hard to separate the teachings from the teachers who have become ensnared in these traps. Students unfortunately often tend to throw out the baby (the teachings) with the bath water (the teacher) when they become aware that their teacher has been engaged in harmful or non-ethical activities.

But the interesting thing in my case was that even before the proverbial shit hit the fan with my teacher, I remember feeling embarrassed to speak about him to people who were not also part of his group, even though I knew I was learning a great deal from him and waking up to experiences beyond any imaginings I'd ever had of spiritual realities. I felt I should have been able to learn all I was learning on my own.

And then, after I learned he had done any number of awful things to certain people, I felt especially embarrassed that I could have been "taken in" by him. It was really difficult for me (and many others who left the group at the same time) to put the powerful teachings we'd received through this teacher together with the man, himself.

Like many others I've since known who have been disillusioned by spiritual teachers, I experienced painful feelings of confusion, hurt and anger. He was an extremely accurate psychic and therefore easy to give power to. And those who had surrendered a lot of their own inner authority felt the disillusionment especially hard.

What made it all the more confusing for me was an incredible lucid, out-of-body experience I had with him one night in the sleep state after I'd left his group. In this experience he and I were walking along a path, literally all night long, arm in arm, talking.

When I woke up the next morning I couldn't remember the exact conversation we'd had, but I was still experiencing the enormous love that was present between us in that experience.

I understood when I woke up that the third-dimensional energies here on the planet—especially back then—were just too much for him to do the job he'd taken on in as clear a manner as he'd hoped. I also realized that he'd probably accrued a whole lot of karma he'd have to balance at some point later on. I felt an enormous compassion for him. And any anger, disillusionment, and blame I'd been feeling simply vanished with these realizations.

Since then I have always cautioned people who have had similar disillusionments about spiritual teachers they've been with that these situations are never as black and white as they may seem.

Before incarnation, Souls can have plans to attempt to serve as spiritual teachers with the greatest and purest of intentions. But once they get here and encounter all that the Third and Fourth Dimensions have to challenge them with, they can sometimes fall short dramatically in their intentions. Being a spiritual teacher is not an easy task to take on. The ego can be such a skillful and stealthy manipulator—especially so the more awake we become.

Awakening with a Guru

About ten years later, after a period in which I felt inwardly guided to just be on my own spiritually and not follow any particular teacher or teachings, I again felt drawn in by another teacher.

This one was the Indian guru known as Papaji. I initially resisted him, not only because of my experience with my former teacher, but because I felt it was step up to go from a spiritual teacher to a guru. Gurus often talk about our needing to surrender to them—and the very thought of this was anathema to me.

I therefore resisted his pull for a while, even though after simply reading a book of his teachings, I was having incredible inner experiences of a sort I'd never encountered before. But he would often appear to me clearly in meditation and say with deep love, "Come home, Child." It would bring me to tears. I would experience an intense longing to "go home"—and I'd feel this feeling of home present with him.

At some point after reading the first book about him, I had the profound enlightenment awakening I described in Chapter 2, and I knew he had somehow helped to "orchestrate" this occurrence in me. My gratitude for him was enormous, my love beyond any love I'd ever experienced before for a teacher. I could only speak of this love to those who had also had a life-changing relationship with a guru and knew that the guru-devotee relationship was in a class of its own.

Yet even with this experience, it took me two years before I overcame my resistance to his pull inside me (as well as my resistance to going to India, a country I just didn't feel drawn to)—and I went to see him.

I can't find words to fully describe my experience with him when I was finally before him and looking into his eyes. I don't generally see anything with my eyes open that isn't present physically. But I suddenly clearly saw clear golden streams of love emanating from his eyes that were flowing directly into my heart. My whole body responded with deep reverberations, creating a deep opening to receive this love.

And in a single moment, I realized that I had literally lived lifetimes waiting for this moment with him. I was struck mute—I couldn't speak at all when he asked me a question. I simply stared at him and then collapsed in a heap at his feet, sobbing.

That night, all night long in the sleep state, I danced with him. The love connection I shared with him had been anchored so deeply within me, it was as if I was a part of him, and he a part of me—there was no division. We were two halves of a whole.

A year later, I had another out-of-body experience with him. And this time, much to my amazement, I was following after him on my hands and knees, actually kissing the ground he'd been walking on. I've got to say that, even after the experience I'd had with him in India, to even think about doing something like kissing the ground someone had walked on was an idea that was completely alien to me.

I am not naturally what is known as a "bhakti"—a person who finds loving devotion to a teacher to be their path of awakening. As a born-and-bred Westerner with independence drilled into me since childhood—along with all my resistances to teachers, to begin with—wanting to kiss the ground some man had walked on was not a feeling that was at all natural for me. And yet here I was in this experience, doing it with a profound reverence for the Grace I knew he embodied.

I have never lost the knowing of who Papaji was for me or my love for him. And yet, at some point, it was time for me to move on again on my awakening path. And I turned inward for another fifteen years or so, moving along on my own inner guidance. Once in a while I would sit with certain teachers and would be very grateful for what they were offering; but for the most part, I stayed with my own inner teachings.

Teachers who Bring us to our Knees

Then along came a man I was again totally surprised to be drawn to as a teacher—the quantum healer I mentioned in Chapter 3 who was known as the "cowboy healer".

Dell Morris was a most unusual man, in that he actually was a cowboy: he spoke like one, in certain ways acted like one, and had lived his life as one. He was someone who, on the physical personality level, I couldn't relate to at all. And yet I knew deep inside me I was there to learn whatever he could teach me. It was what was "next" for me on my path.

Among other things, he was a phenomenal healer—but perhaps, even more importantly for me, it was clear that he knew from direct experience what the Fifth Dimension was all about. And he was offering an intensive program for moving into that reality which really spoke to me.

I also decided to work with him because, after so many years of simply moving very gradually into full awakening, I realized I was tired of how slowly the process was unfolding. I wanted to work through whatever was standing in my way as quickly as I could. And he came through with what he promised. I began doing the deep spiritual work required in his programs. And I almost immediately started awakening to aspects of my higher self I'd never been acquainted with before.

But this was a teacher who went for my jugular. He brought me to my knees. I fought and argued with him, both in my head and occasionally out loud with him. I didn't like his style of teaching, I didn't like how he treated me; I thought he was unduly harsh with people.

But in the end, before he left the planet, I realized what a gift he had given me in helping me to break down the hardened egoic walls that had surrounded me. As much as I didn't like what he had dished out to me or how he'd done it, I knew it was probably exactly what I needed.

And now, when I tune into him since his death, especially when I offer to others the healing work I learned from him, I feel him immeasurably close and accessible to me. And there is an enormous love and understanding we share.

He's another teacher I've had an experience with while in the sleep state: we spent a long sojourn together one night, all night long. In the experience, at times I would feel myself just wanting to fall asleep (even though, yes, I was already asleep—we all know the irrationality of these experiences!) and I would just kind of lean against him in a most comfortable, familiar way and drift off. We were old, old friends. Little would I ever have expected to have this kind of experience with the man I had internally struggled with during much of my time with him while he was alive.

It wasn't as if I had never experienced love for him while he was alive—I actually did. A lot of love as well as enormous gratitude. But somehow the love I've now experienced on the inner realms since his death is so much more profound, pure, and real.

When we have these kinds of experiences on the higher dimensions with teachers we've had, the true nature of both our teachers and our relationships with them are revealed. Just like with other people, our actual relationship with them can be hidden from us until we experience them in a higher vibrational plane. When we meet them there, we find that all there really is between us is love.

Experiencing Ourselves as Love

It's very exciting for me to see all my relationships transforming during these times, as I've described. I could say I've worked very hard to transform myself and this is one of the results of that work. But this is only partially true.

My sense is that something is dramatically shifting within all of us around our ability to experience love. Old distorted views and experiences of it are leaving, and new clarity is moving in. Opportunities for experiencing ever deeper love abound.

We are beginning to experience ourselves *as* love and to realize that, in the end, this is all that really matters.

Chapter 8

Learning to Love Ourselves

As may be evident, full and complete self-love is a prerequisite for entering the Fifth Dimension. We cannot move into this high vibration with any sense of self-judgment or self-rejection we're still holding onto.

Unfortunately, learning how to love ourselves is one of the most difficult things to learn. Many of us have worked hard at this over the years, and we still have not been totally successful in achieving it. And some of us aren't yet aware that this is at the core of our suffering and demands to be met if we are to fully awaken to who we are.

Part of the problem has been getting past the conditioning in the collective consciousness we all live in that judges the notion of self-love as "selfish" or "self-absorbed". Even many so-called spiritual teachings frown on the idea of focusing on our need to love ourselves, teaching instead that loving, forgiving and serving others is what's most important.

Many of us who have been on a path of self-discovery and healing for a long time have been able to get past those attitudes and have been able to focus on exploring what it means to love ourselves unconditionally. However, to even understand what loving ourselves is about isn't a simple matter. What does it entail exactly? And how do we go about it?

What is the "Self" We Need to Love?

When we seriously contemplate loving ourselves, a lot of questions can come up. For instance, what exactly is the "self" we need to love? Does loving ourselves mean we love everything we do? All our attitudes and judgments? Do we have to love our bodies? Do we need to love all our emotions, all our pain? Do we have to *like* ourselves? Does it mean we just learn to love our Soul or our "True Self"? (And if so, then exactly what is *that*?)

And even if we were to finally understand that it probably includes *all* of this—then how do we go about learning how to love it all, if we have judgments and difficult emotions attached to so much of who we experience ourselves to be?

Many of us on a spiritual path have been taught that we need to first heal ourselves—all our past woundings and all our negative core beliefs about ourselves. And to do this, we've learned that we need to first get in touch with these woundings and beliefs, re-experience all the emotions involved—and then bring in love, understanding, and compassion for ourselves.

There is much to be said for methods that approach healing in this way; they can be helpful. But unfortunately, underneath much of this kind of work lies an assumption that we're somehow broken. And that we need to fix and improve ourselves.

That underlying premise often brings up a sense of unworthiness (or it's added to the one that's already present): the notion that we are not okay with all the unhealed emotions, experiences and memories still alive within us. We need to get rid of them in order to be okay.

Even in many of the teachings about spiritual awakening available (as opposed to ones focusing more on psychological personal growth), there is a similar premise: that not yet being awake is not okay. We need to wake up, and keep waking up more until we're finally "fully awake", before we can be okay.

To get there, we have to keep "growing", meditating, doing spiritual exercises, letting go of the ego, and disciplining ourselves to keep on our path—or we won't be successful in achieving what we're seeking. It can be an insidious message that finds its way into our consciousness, adding to the beliefs and feelings of self-blame and unworthiness that are already there.

Building Ourselves up vs Tearing Ourselves Down

This old third-dimensional paradigm of spirituality essentially focuses on tearing ourselves down. If we really look at it, we can see that whether it's about getting rid of illusion, the ego, or conditioned belief patterns, the tearing down process mainly serves to keep us feeling unworthy and continually "working" on ourselves.

The new Ascension paradigm we are now invited to step into offers us a more profound transformation by building ourselves up. We can discover that rather than always focusing on processing, resolving, and fixing, it's the action of validating ourselves that raises our vibration, brings healing, and ultimately calls out our most awakened qualities.

The most direct and basic thing we can do to raise our vibration is to practice experiencing love for ourselves as often as possible. This invites us to move into love for whatever arises within us— *everything* that appears, pleasant or unpleasant, "spiritual" or "unspiritual".

If we cannot initially love something that arises in us, we can at least learn to simply allow it to be. Rather than resisting it or trying to change it, we can consider accepting it as just what is currently present. When we do this with a sense of surrender, a feeling of compassion can then arise within us, assisting us to love what we have not previously wanted to exist. And we can then feel the freedom that arises with this.

Another approach to keeping our vibration high through an intention to love ourselves is staying focused on what we're doing right, rather than wrong, in every moment. This is so simple, and yet it is very foreign to many. In essence, it's about staying positive about ourselves, no matter what we may be doing or experiencing. It's about looking for what is good in ourselves, even if it's simply an attitude of wanting to do something "right".

Often we have to look past our actions to our intentions or desire to find what is lovable. It can be hard at times to look past the judgment people often have about intentions not counting if the action is "wrong". Yes, this can be helpful to someone who is consistently trying to slide by, not taking responsibility for their actions. Or someone who is stuck in an ego-aggrandizing mode.

But this is rarely the case with people who are conscientiously attempting to move forward on their spiritual path. I'd say that generally, as a group, it is important for us to stay focused on our intentions, as they are more often than not based in love and kindness. And our focus on these intentions can set us onto a path of being gentle with ourselves—which in turn, will motivate our actions in the direction of love.

Letting Go of Self-Judgment

Another very important way to cultivate a love for ourselves is by focusing on letting go of self-judgment. I've found both for myself and for clients I've worked with over the years that this is perhaps the most difficult part of learning to love ourselves—how to shift past the insidious and seemingly unmovable tendency to judge ourselves.

This is especially difficult for those of us who received a lot of judgment and criticism as children. We have "introjected" these negative attitudes we received from parents and other authority figures as children into our adult minds, creating a powerful superego or inner critic.

For most of us, this inner voice can initially be difficult to distinguish from what we actually know rationally about ourselves. When it speaks, it seems to be telling us the truth about ourselves; and if we're not conscious about what it actually is (a mechanism that has incorporated memories of judgments and criticisms we heard and felt as children), it can dominate how we feel about ourselves and guide most of our actions. It operates very powerfully beneath our conscious awareness.

It's important to understand that this voice is not an intelligent consciousness of some kind in our head. It's more like a machine that's been programmed to tell us that we're not good enough, we're not worthy of what we want, and we never will be—no matter what we do. It's automatic and rarely seems to vary its messages about certain subjects. And there is usually an uncomfortable emotional-body response that accompanies its messages.

Sometimes it's hard to know whether what we're internally hearing is coming from this superego or inner critic speaking—or if it's from our intuition. One way to tell is that the superego is always judgmental and fear-based. Intuition is not fear-based; it can give us warning about something, but there's a different feeling that is experienced with the warning. Intuition carries an energy that is loving and protective, rather than one of criticism or punishment.

Speaking Back to the Superego

Once we become conscious of the voice of the inner critic and recognize what it is, we can then begin to catch it and deal with it.

There are various techniques that I've found effective in working with it, once we are determined to begin wresting control from it.

One is to simply respond forcibly to the voice of the inner critic when we hear it. For instance, if we hear, "Oh I can't do that—I'm not smart enough (strong enough, attractive enough, spiritual enough, etc.), we can simply tell it with energy and authority to shut up.

This can be a very effective way of abruptly stopping the voice in its tracks. A very pleasant silence can follow this response in which a feeling of empowerment may arise. Then we can counter the voice by stating the opposite of what we've heard, what we know in our adult mind to be true about ourselves.

One "Shut up!" will not usually do it, however. It entails a process of keeping alert to the superego voice and actively countering it over and over again before you can start feeling some peace about certain judgments you've had about yourself.

Taking Charge

At one point, I came up with an alternate method of dealing with the inner critic. I used it for many years with myself and also with a number of clients who used it with varying degrees of success. It involved picturing the inner critic as a part of a "family" inside of me. I saw it as an old, crotchety woman who was bossy and constantly judgmental and complaining (kind of a cartoon caricature of my mother).

Within this "family", I was a single mother with a child (my inner child). And I was also responsible for the care of this old woman. I had become aware that I had allowed this old woman to constantly run her mouth at both my child and me my whole life, and it was time to stop this. I needed to step into my power as the head of this household and let her know who was boss.

My first task was to get her off of my child's back. I realized how painful it was for my child whenever I'd catch the old woman's voice criticizing us. So, with strong intention, I'd move into my center of power and confront her, demanding firmly that she stop her criticizing. I'd speak with the energy of a lioness protecting her cub, telling her that I simply wouldn't allow her to speak that way to my child anymore.

She was startled to be spoken to like that and she'd just go silent. The emotional response of relief in my inner child to this

endously impactful. Once the old woman was silent, I'd
to my child and speak words of comfort, surrounding her
with my protective love.

It got to be kind of fun. I found myself warning this old woman
that if she didn't stop her criticizing, she'd need to go into her room
and stay there with the door shut. I'd tell her that I'd bring her
dinner, and let her watch TV if she wanted—but she wouldn't be
allowed to spend time with my child and me for a while until she
could behave with kindness and respect.

I knew it was important to speak with firm authority to her, but
also a sense of calm compassion. She would always reluctantly
realize that I was inherently the boss in the household and that I
was finally stepping into that role. And it would always effectively
shut her up—at least for a while.

During these times, I could feel a sense of trust developing in my
inner child toward me. I also had good practice in shifting from a
mode of victimhood into a sense of claiming my own power and
taking charge of what occurred within my consciousness. It kept
me more conscious and alert than I had ever been about what was
happening inside my head. Until then, I had truly been at the mercy
of a powerful inner critic that I had unconsciously allowed to run
me my whole life.

Practicing this awareness through this "household" scenario
helped greatly to lessen the impact of the inner critic within me. Its
voice got weaker and weaker and eventually there were no longer
any words it would use. It became simply a sensation, a feeling that
would occasionally occur that I'd recognize as the ghost of that
crotchety, critical old woman.

The Out-Picturing of an Inner Dynamic

It was during these times also that I experienced
synchronistically an out-picturing of the inner scenario I was
practicing. My mother, whom I had always experienced as very
critical—and had become ever more crotchety in her elder years—
invited my teenage daughter and me on a trip to France.

Poor dear—she was miserable for a myriad of reasons
throughout the entire three weeks we were together. She wasn't
happy about any of the accommodations we had booked or just
about anything my daughter and I did. A constant stream of
complaints issued from her the whole trip.

The important thing was how she would consistently put me in a double-bind situation, in which there was no way I could win: I'd always be the one who was guilty of causing her unhappiness. Whichever option she'd give me, I'd lose. It was wonderful to see because it became extremely clear to me that this is what I'd grown up with.

Because of the inner work I'd done with my own version of her inside of me with my "inner family", I was finally able to step free of her attempts to manipulate me through guilt. On several occasions, instead of reacting to her with either guilt or resentment, I moved into a new place of empowerment with her and refused both of the losing options she was giving me. Instead, with total equanimity, I took responsibility for deciding my own course of action, gently but firmly placing her unhappiness back in her own lap.

She actually pouted for entire days after I'd do this, not speaking to us. But she finally realized her guilt trips (all unconscious, I'm sure) simply weren't working anymore and she eventually began speaking to us again. It was enormously empowering for me, as I realized I had finally stepped into my own inner authority with her. I felt no anger toward her anymore—only compassion.

It was also important for me to realize that it did me no good to blame my mother for how she treated me, either as a child or as an adult. She was only doing the best she could—given that she too, I knew, had a very powerful superego with which she was always dealing. I was also very grateful for how she eventually helped me to step into my own power.

It further became clear to me in reflecting on this whole process with her, how the inner critic is also responsible for turning criticism and blame outward—not just inwardly toward ourselves. When it gets too painful for us hearing judgment turned toward ourselves, we use this same mechanism to project judgment and blame outside ourselves toward other people.

At any rate, the outer experience I had with my mother when I finally took charge and assumed responsibility for my own actions and decisions further enhanced the work I'd inwardly done with my inner critic. Its voice became simply a feeling or a subtle impulse I could sense from time to time.

Inhabiting the "Center of Your Head"

Nonetheless, much to my consternation, I found that the superego was still there, however subtle its voice now was. No matter what I did or what happened in my life, it seemed this inner critic voice remained within me. It was puzzling.

Eventually, I read about a tool that teacher Jim Self offers as a way to deal with it. He refers to it as the voice of "mother-father-teacher-minister" and says it lives in the "center" of our head. The key to working with it is to be aware of its presence there and to move it out by consciously inhabiting that place in our head ourselves.

When I first heard this, I knew he was on to something— because the inner critic had always felt like it was right there in the center of my head. But I also believed I was already inhabiting that part of my head, along with that voice, so I was confused.

Yet when I really tuned into that space in my head, I realized I actually *wasn't* in there. Somehow, my awareness was outside of my head—or somewhere else in my head. That center space, right behind my eyes and slightly above, was a place I'd never really fully inhabited.

In following the instructions to move into that space, I found it very satisfying to claim my rightful place in my head. As I consciously moved my awareness there, probably for the first time ever, I felt the inner critic being pushed outside of me. There was no room for it with me in there.

It was as if I was finally claiming my natural inheritance as "queen" inside my own consciousness. It was extremely powerful— and continues to be, any time I realize the inner critic might be subtly trying to reclaim its position back in my head.

These particular techniques probably won't work for everyone. But it seems important that we all find something that does work to bring the inner critic mechanism into our awareness so we can learn how to work with it and eventually claim our freedom from it.

I find that the inner critic is probably responsible for all our difficulties in fully feeling compassion for ourselves. If we pay attention to it, we can see that it is responsible for all judgments we have about ourselves—about our actions, our emotions, our thoughts, the way our body looks, how awake we are (or aren't).

It keeps us busy trying endlessly to "improve" ourselves. Although this can be somewhat helpful in the early days of waking up—after a while, we can see that there is no end to the criticism and push to be someone "better" than who we are. It keeps us caught in the mire of unworthiness—one of the hallmarks of third-dimensional consciousness.

The Controllers

What occurs to me is that this superego voice has probably been inherent in the human psyche for eons—likely since the Fall of Consciousness. It seems to be a collective phenomenon, not so much a personal one.

There are those who speak about the "Controllers", the "Archons", or the "Reptile Race"—powerful negative beings who evidently found their way into the Earth's atmosphere from other galaxies long, long ago and have essentially ruled this planet and kept the human race in submission through certain humans in their control for many thousands of years.

According to some sources, one way they initially assumed their power is through instilling a mechanism (the superego) in the human psyche that was not part of the original human design. Other sources suggest they inserted implants into the design that would pervert the function of the superego. Either way, this has kept humanity in fear and with a sense of unworthiness all this time.

Although this sounds like science fiction or conspiracy-type thinking—or simply too ridiculous or fantastical to consider as reality—I have to say, that despite the fact that I initially rejected the whole idea, it's always rung true for me.

I generally don't like focusing on negative scenarios like this. But intuitively, I've always sensed the truth in the idea that there has been a dynamic of control and suppression of the human race by a very small elite group of people that's been going on for a long time. Because most of us can't remember a time when it wasn't happening, we've just always assumed this is "just the way life is".

What I find interesting is that although the noted spiritual teacher Hameed Ali doesn't speak about any of this, he does address the superego in a similar manner in his Diamond Heart teachings. Most of the approach of these teachings is to fully embrace every facet of ourselves—including everything we consider a flaw or imperfection—as well as our true divine nature. We must learn to love *all* of who we are.

There is one exception he makes: the superego. He says this is one aspect of the human psyche we must always reject and resist. Again, this brings to mind the thought that this aspect within us is not natural—it was not originally part of our design as humans.

Unworthiness is on its Way Out

Whatever the truth about any of this may be, in the end it probably doesn't really matter. I do believe that the sense of unworthiness in the human collective will in time no longer exist within us; the superego will be gone. It's simply not part of fifth-dimensional consciousness. There is no place for it. In the Fifth Dimension, we naturally stand in our own authority, knowing who we truly are as magnificent and powerful multi-dimensional beings.

And many of us are already having experiences of this consciousness. There's a clear knowing of our inherent majesty and power into which we're now stepping. It is our natural inheritance. The veils of forgetfulness are dropping and we're remembering who we are. All the old ways of striving for perfection and struggling to wake up seem to be diminishing.

This is all coming about, I believe, due to the new Ascension energies on the planet that are gently nudging us in the direction of loving ourselves without constraint or conditions. We seem to be understanding more quickly these days what loving ourselves means—and we're able to let go of old attitudes of having to change ourselves first.

We're realizing that there is no need to earn love or deserve it. There's no need to do hard work to learn how to love ourselves. We don't need to "grow" into something more. A new and higher energy is pushing its way into all of our hearts, whether we're aware of it or not.

It's a matter of seeing and then releasing all old distorted third-dimensional misperceptions of who we are—and step into our inner authority, realizing who we've been all along.

Shift in Self-Love

As is perhaps evident in these writings, I have worked hard during my life toward developing a greater love for myself. For a long time it was difficult to find a compassion for myself and to embrace myself unconditionally just as I was.

Having perfectionism and inadequacy as core traits in my personality, I had to consistently catch myself in my self-judgments and try to talk myself into accepting who I was and what I did. Over time I learned to forgive myself, not push myself toward perfection all the time, and to choose to fully accept myself even with what I considered my "faults" or "weaknesses".

I soon learned that this needed to be a constant practice; and although it brought about a greater sense of compassion for myself when I could achieve it, it felt like an ongoing kind of task I needed to be on top of all the time. The inherent drive toward self-judgment and pushing to be perfect continued to be powerful, despite all the work I'd done in this area of my personality.

The difference I see now, after a few years into the Ascension process, is that the self-judgment is no longer my default attitude toward myself. It still appears in an anemic form once in a while, just out of habit. What has replaced it is an attitude of both really liking and loving myself.

It gradually became a surprise to me to discover at one point that I rarely felt that I simply *liked* myself. This was a revelation. After all the years I had lived with myself, how could I not have liked myself? But it was true. There was always enough automatic criticism of myself present, that liking and respecting myself was not a natural feeling.

Yet now it is. And I don't think this is because I've become a more likable person. There's just an absence of the old self-judgment that was always there. So it feels easy and natural to simply both like and love myself. I see clearly all the aspects of myself that are truly valuable and lovable.

There are other times when the whole notion of "likable" and "unlikable", and "lovable" and "unlovable" simply vanishes. This is when I see the different aspects of my personality from a totally neutral point of view—neither good nor bad, attractive nor unattractive. I just notice qualities there that may be different from what I've always liked or what I observe in other people—but there's no judging or comparison going on.

This perspective feels as if it's coming from an even higher source than seeing all the "good" qualities I happen to like or value about myself. There's nothing there to defend, change, or focus on. I just am what I am, unique in how I am personally constructed. And since, when I am experiencing this perspective of myself, I am generally filled with an inherent love for everything that appears in life, I am naturally filled with a love for myself.

When I'm in this state of consciousness, I don't have to avoid self-judgment or consciously choose to be supportive and compassionate with myself all the time. There's generally nothing present that's either self-judgment or self-compassion.

I see that love and compassion are woven into the very fabric of everything that exists. Judgment and criticism simply aren't there. I feel empty and free—neutral about all human qualities.

Discovering Love Rather than Developing It

I believe that rather than struggling to create or develop love for myself, I have rather *discovered* it. It has always naturally been here in me; I've simply blocked it with self-judgments and a belief that I've needed to change myself in order to be lovable. Once I dropped the judgments and belief, what I found was that love for myself was just there waiting for me to discover it.

I believe that love is naturally at the core of our being. It's our essential nature—not something that's separate from us or added onto us. It's the primal essence of all of life. We can stop trying to develop or create it, and instead discover it to be who we *are.*

Making Decisions Based in Self-Love

Through this recent time I've found an increasing number of people I work with are discovering that learning to love themselves is central to their Ascension process. Indeed, for many, a lack of self-love seems to be the one block on their spiritual journey that stands in their way of stepping free from suffering.

I encourage them to be alert to their simple, everyday decisions in their lives, as well as the more important ones. I suggest they ask a question whenever they're making a decision: *Is this decision based in self-love?*

A young man recently reported to me: "Until I started watching myself closely, I never realized how often I just automatically make decisions based on what I think will make someone else happy. It doesn't even occur to me to ask myself if it's something *I* might want."

If we're being motivated by self-judgment or self-doubt, or meeting someone else's expectations, our decision cannot be of the highest vibration. We will be effectively lowering our vibration.

Making decisions based in loving ourselves and taking good care of ourselves on every level always ensures that we are moving ourselves forward on our path to a higher dimension. This demands an attuned and constant awareness in most of us—as third-dimensional habit patterns can be very powerful.

But with constant alertness to our inner processes and an intention to act out of love for ourselves, it can become easier to make it a habit. And with this habit, our journey into the Fifth Dimension is both accelerated and made smoother.

Chapter 9

Letting Go of 3D Habit Patterns

It can be discouraging to see what continues to occur in the world, when we can so clearly imagine a possible world in which love and harmony reign. Indeed, it can seem as if we're all still living in the Third Dimension. War, injustice, and greed are all still so prevalent.

And, at least occasionally, it may feel as if *we* are still living in 3D, as well. Although we may be well aware of the Shift taking place within and around us, our old ways of operating can still feel like they're in place. We continue to fall into fear, anger and depression at times.

As I've stated earlier, we are no longer living in third-dimensional reality; that reality closed off on the Earth back in December 2012. The rigid and limiting structures of that dimension are no longer in operation. However, most people in the world—and even many of us who know better—can find we are still functioning as if those old confining structures continue to exist.

Operating in the Fourth Dimension

What is now in place and what we can operate from is a new structure of reality: the Fourth Dimension, which is the bridge from the rigid third-dimensional consciousness into a new, open, and fully-conscious fifth-dimensional consciousness.

And although this new Fourth Dimension reality is not as open and free as that of the Fifth Dimension, it is not as limiting or rigid as the Third Dimension was. Everything in 4D is energetically looser, freer. We are not so confined and enslaved to lower energetic frequencies. New and empowering frequencies streaming onto the Earth are available to us. We are capable now of consciously creating our own reality.

In this new 4D reality, among other things, we can become aware that linear time is collapsing, and time can actually stretch and compress. We now have the time and capacity to shift our negative reactions to people and events; we can choose within a moment to not react out of fear, hurt or anger. We can actually change reality through choice and intention. And we can also see that manifestation is happening much more quickly.

Shifting From 3D Habit Patterns

The problem is most people don't know that the rules have changed in this new dimension and they continue to operate from old 3D habit patterns in how they go about their lives. But those of us who know reality is shifting can understand this and challenge and release the habit patterns we've brought with us from living in the Third Dimension. We can develop new habits based on 5D understandings.

However, this is not a simple matter for most of us. We all have deeply-embedded, erroneous beliefs about reality and about ourselves that we bring with us from living many thousands of years in the Third Dimension, beliefs that underlie all the many distortions and disinformation that have caused humans suffering throughout the ages. These beliefs naturally color our experiences and perceptions of life in unconscious ways.

As such, for most of us to truly shift these deeply-ingrained beliefs, it is necessary to have a strong intention to first of all explore and discover what our limited, distorted and erroneous beliefs are. Then we need to do whatever is necessary to see through them and replace them with beliefs that reflect a higher truth.

Although 4D energies are helping to facilitate this process in us, many of our 3D beliefs are buried so deeply in our cellular, mental and emotional dimensions that it requires awareness, intention, and some focused work to let go of them.

The following are common 3D beliefs and habit patterns that I find many of us are still holding onto and operating from.

Believing We're the Body-Mind

Even if we've had numerous profound experiences of being a vast, multi-dimensional being—or of knowing ourselves simply as Awareness—it can be easy to fall into the habit pattern of believing that we are merely the small body-mind being we experienced ourselves to be when totally engulfed in third-dimensional reality.

Recognizing that we're operating from this erroneous belief can help to shift our awareness to the expanded reality of who we are. A sense of relief and liberation can flow in, helping us to experience ourselves more clearly as a spiritual being temporarily experiencing ourselves through dense human form.

Many of us have spent years of spiritual practice in pursuit of the experience and actual knowing of this truth that we are much more than the body-mind. And we have at least had glimpses of that reality. Yet it is perhaps the most difficult 3D belief to overcome.

If being more than the body-mind is still only a mental concept for you and not an actual experience or knowing, I invite you to bring the idea into your meditations and/or spiritual inquiry sessions. In my experience, the realization that we are so much more than what we perceive on the physical level can be one of the most liberating experiences with which we can be graced. And it is an important doorway into discovering who we are as a fifth-dimensional Consciousness.

Believing We Need to Worry about Survival

We may balk at hearing that survival fear is only a 3D worry. We don't want to be unrealistic; we still need to have money coming in to provide for shelter, food, and all the rest that's necessary to keep us alive. Of course.

The belief I'm pointing to is the one that tells us we have to *worry* or be concerned about our survival. It's a belief most of us have inherited from childhood, that we have to struggle and work hard in order to survive, and that it's reasonable to panic when we don't see how it's going to happen. It's based on a belief that the universe is an unfriendly and unsupportive place.

If we can have the courage to truly trust that the Divine will always provide for us, then we are operating in fifth-dimensional reality. In 5D consciousness we know we are not meant to struggle for survival. The only thing that keeps us in the struggle is a belief that we have to stay in that struggle in order to survive. Abundance truly is available to every one of us, if we can change our beliefs around it and our sense of worth.

If you have had to deal with concerns about your financial survival in your life, moving into this higher consciousness and developing new beliefs can be challenging. One way to approach the matter is to look back at your life and become aware of the times in the past you have felt fearful about survival.

If you're like most people in this position, you can probably think of times when unexpected things happened that "saved" you financially. Each time you managed to land back on your feet and were able to carry on.

Contrary to what your fearful belief may be telling you, the Universe truly has innumerable ways in which it can provide for you. Having a job is only one way.

Believing We're Unworthy

Believing we're unworthy is a belief that is often unconscious, but it lurks within many of our psyches. There's a sense that happiness, wealth and well-being are things that need to be earned; our worth has to be proven before we can be awarded what we need in order to feel happy and fulfilled.

This belief seems to be quite prevalent among lightworkers. Many of us have been on the Earth since very ancient times and have had innumerable lifetimes in the Third Dimension, in which every effort we made to move forward in consciousness was met with some kind of resistance or punishment, leading us to believe we were not inherently worthy.

A nagging sense of unworthiness can be tough to overcome. It seems to be ingrained very deeply in so many of us. But again, if we can become aware of this belief when it arises within us and how it's producing unwanted results in our lives, we can begin the process of short-circuiting it.

We need to see it clearly as a strongly-conditioned belief and know that it's not truth. Who we are, just as we are, does not have to change in any way whatsoever for us to be worthy of well-being, wealth, happiness and good health. It is our divine inheritance as Souls. We now need to claim it.

Getting Caught up in the World's Suffering

Most lightworkers I know are empathic and compassionate people, and have often taken on the world's woes. It might feel selfish to not become focused on or worried about people across the world who have just experienced a devastating earthquake or about the sea animals caught up in oil spills. We may feel guilty, as well, that we ourselves are living in relative ease and comfort.

Concern and distress are signs of compassion and deep connection with other beings. They're important. They help to fully open our hearts. We are indeed connected with all beings on this Earth—and with the Earth itself—and we can feel this connection deeply within our hearts.

But this does not mean we need to experience depression, anger or grief when others do. We do not have to suffer along with them. In fact, if we dwell on these emotions—no matter how compassionate they may feel—we are actually adding to the problem. We have joined in the lower vibration of suffering and have added that vibration to the collective that is experiencing the suffering we're wishing to alleviate.

Of course, if we feel drawn to actually contribute something constructive or helpful to those in need, then we can be helpful in raising their vibration, especially if we do it with love, joy and optimism. Those emotions have a powerful impact on sorrow. Suffering along with someone dealing with misfortune does not assist them.

What is infinitely more valuable is to continue living our lives from within a "5D bubble" we've created, in which we can remain in a mood of joy, optimism, love and harmony, no matter what. Indeed, this is what can assist the entire human race to shift into the very same higher vibration.

Keeping Ourselves Small

I find that many of us are fearful of stepping into our full power. There's a tendency to keep ourselves small, blending in with others in a group, in order to stay in a position that feels safe. There's a fear that if we were to be out there demonstrating fully who we are and offering what we know, we might somehow be punished or rejected.

If we find ourselves trying to keep invisible, it's important to see if we can recognize this as an old 3D habit pattern. Many of us have lived lifetimes in which we were indeed not only punished for fully expressing who we were, we were often tortured and put to death. It's just what happened during the really dark times we lived through in the Third Dimension.

But the truth is that we are no longer there. We're in a time now—especially in the developed West—in which it is much safer to express ourselves as the powerful and awake beings that we are. And, indeed, the world at this time really needs us to do just that.

We need to see the pull to not make waves as a subconscious habit that no longer serves us or the world. We need to trust that coming out and being as big and empowered as we can be will not only be safe, it will greatly raise our own vibration as well as that of the collective.

Yes, it's important to not do this through ego motivation; but it's not likely we're going to do that at this point in our evolution, so long as we keep asking for inner guidance and pray for clarity. And we can move forward with small, gradual steps into the full expression of who we are. We may not always be welcomed by everyone we meet. But we shouldn't let that stop us. Our being fully who we are is what is needed both for ourselves and for the world.

Focusing on What's Wrong with Us

As I've mentioned earlier, another 3D habit I often see in many of us is keeping focused on what's wrong with ourselves and what we need to "fix". Many of the third-dimensional paths of self-improvement and spirituality—although helpful to us in past decades—have unfortunately fostered this approach to awakening. It was helpful in pointing to, and often in releasing, the reasons we were not awake or happy. But this approach seldom directly brings about either awakening or happiness. It can actually drag down our self-esteem and confidence—and thus our vibration.

If we find ourselves caught in this habit pattern of focusing on what's wrong with us, we need to try instead to begin paying attention to what is right with us, to focus on the qualities in ourselves we've decided are "good" or "spiritual". And to also concentrate on what is working well in our lives, rather on what feels like it's going wrong.

Because the habit of looking at what's wrong can be so ingrained, at first this approach of looking at what's right can feel Pollyannaish or unrealistic. We need to remember that this in itself is a 3D belief.

Focusing on the positive is actually natural when we're in 5D consciousness. In this higher vibration, we can realize how intelligent it is to keep our attention on the positive. Not only does it help us to feel better about ourselves in the moment, it actually has the power to create a more positive reality for us by telling the universe we desire more of this positive experience in our life. It helps to remember that whatever we focus on, that's what we magnetize and create.

Creating New 5D Habits

New habits are not always easy to create. If the old habits are well-ingrained and held in place by strong beliefs, we have to keep vigilant and keep watch on the automatic decisions we make on a daily basis.

When making a decision, we can ask ourselves:

> ➤ Am I deciding to do this out of fear of not being safe? Or not being loved?
> ➤ Am I acting out of self-judgment?
> ➤ Am I doing this based on self-doubt?
> ➤ Am I forgetting who I really am and the power I have?

Fully letting go of 3D habit patterns takes some work and attention, and it's definitely a process. But it's essential to pay attention to this as we progress further along on our Ascension paths.

As we will discover, we cannot take our 3D "baggage" with us into the Fifth Dimension. However, we have a choice as to how we're going to let go of this baggage before we arrive there. We can allow life to teach us the hard way through loss and other difficult experiences. Or we can make a decision to focus now on our 3D habit patterns and beliefs and consciously work to let go of them. We can have the intention to adopt beliefs and ways of functioning that align us more fully with fifth-dimensional consciousness.

My experience is that making intentional choices like this can ensure a smoother and more conscious process as we venture forth on our path leading into the Fifth Dimension.

Entering into
Fifth Dimensional Consciousness

Chapter 10

Opening to the Invisible Worlds

In this section relating to entering 5D consciousness, we will begin looking at the positive and exciting experiences many of us are having in our Ascension process—new openings, discoveries, insights and shifts that we're experiencing.

It's important to remember that, along with the many challenges we are facing in our Ascension process, many of us are also having very profound experiences of higher consciousness. Reading about those that I and others I know are having may spark some recognition of experiences you've also been having.

Accessing Inner Guidance

The first area type of experiences I will describe are those in which we are opening ourselves to other realms of existence beyond our physical world that until recently have been invisible and relatively inaccessible to most of us.

Most of us on a conscious spiritual path have learned to tune into what we might call our *inner guidance* when seeking answers to deep questions we have or finding direction in life. Spiritual teachings often direct us to "go within" to get answers.

Yet it's not always easy to do. Often our chattering mind is too loud for us to hear anything beyond it. Or our emotions are too tumultuous. We may not be able to distinguish our inner guidance from the voice of our superego or another inner voice. Much doubt can arise, especially if what we're hearing, feeling or intuiting is not what we would either expect or want to know.

I've found that listening for inner guidance is an art that needs to be practiced again and again before a deep trust in the process can be attained. And then we must develop the courage to *follow* the guidance through action.

There are times when large issues are at stake, and all outer "evidence" is pointing us in one direction—usually to something that is comfortable and familiar from the past. And yet we'll hear from our inner guidance to go in a completely new and unfamiliar direction, leaving us fearful of taking the chance of following it.

Avoiding Lower-Vibrational Entities

Something that comes up for certain people I've worked with is a fear that they might be listening to some lower-vibration entity hovering near them, instead of their higher self or beings they can trust. This is an important concern.

Many of us are very sensitive and open to other realms of existence. And on some of these realms, as I discussed in Chapter 4, there do exist lost, confused or dark entities which attempt to find their way into the auras of embodied human beings. Some are not even human and function in ways that can be rather frightening.

For a number of years, I performed a healing method referred to as *depossession* or *spirit releasement* with certain clients who appeared to have disembodied spirits with them, and I witnessed enormous changes that happened for those people afterwards. So I can attest to the reality of the phenomenon of possession.

It's actually more common than might be expected. Even though I no longer offer that specific kind of work, I do still encounter these types of entities attached to people to whom I currently give healings.

There are people, I've found, who have deceased relatives or other loved ones hanging out in their auras with them—people who for some reason did not move into the higher realms beyond the physical at the time of death. And these entities can quite negatively affect a person in their life, lending a sense of heaviness, anger, fear, depression, or sourness to their personality that wasn't previously there.

These disembodied human entities can be relatively easy to work with and sent on their way through different methods, and it can give a person a great deal of relief to have them gone. If you're concerned about possibly having an entity with you, you can search online under "spirit releasement" to find a practitioner to help you release it. Most of them can work long-distance with people.

What's important to understand about entities is that the person who has had them removed from their aura needs to be highly motivated to do whatever is necessary to not attract them back again. As with all of life, like attracts like. And so if someone continues to feel depressed, angry or highly fearful for any length of time, there is the possibility of attracting entities whose energies match those emotional states.

This is especially true if someone indulges in either alcohol or drugs; taking any substance like this for any length of time creates weaknesses and even holes in the aura and can actually invite in such disembodied spirits. It's therefore very important for people who have had entities removed to not indulge in mind-altering substances—and also to consistently surround themselves with Divine Light, and call in angels, guides and other high-vibrational beings for support, protection and guidance.

The Importance of Discernment

In a certain way, it really isn't so difficult when we're listening for inner guidance to know how to discern where the guidance we're hearing is coming from. In my experience, it really isn't difficult, in that guidance from the higher-vibrational realms is never fear-based. There's generally a feeling of deep love and protectiveness with it, or at least a sense of clear neutrality.

The voice (or it may instead be a thought form—a whole idea rather than words that comes into our awareness) often contains a sensation of a gentle urging. There may also be a body feeling that comes with it, and this is important to pay attention to. If there's a tightening in the gut or chest when we receive the communication, it may not be our inner guidance.

Relationship with Our Spirit Guides

Something I've noticed lately is that people I'm working with are becoming increasingly interested in learning who their guides are and wanting to work with them more closely. I've found that a deep connection with guides can really help people learn to trust the guidance they receive from these beings working closely with them.

Over the years, I've developed a relationship with my guides that has been very helpful to me. Many years ago, when I first began tuning into them, I was particularly interested in getting to know who each of them was, what their names were, what they looked like, and why they were with me. I was fortunate in that they cooperated with my desire, each showing themselves to me, telling me their names and describing their special connection with me or what they were specifically here to assist me with.

For a while, I had dialogues with them often, learning not just about how they were helping me with my life and with spiritual awakening—but also how they themselves functioned. They told me that many of us who are currently embodied have also spent times on the inner realms in between lifetimes as guides to other embodied Souls. That had never occurred to me. But they showed me times when I had served in that way.

Sometimes I had not just been with one human being—I was instead with a group of people who had a purpose to accomplish together. One example was when St. Germaine was energetically guiding the leaders of the American Revolution and the signers of the Declaration of Independence. They showed me that I was privileged to be part of the enormous group of beings on the "Other Side" who assisted him. They said I acted as a kind of "go-for" for the more advanced beings who were doing the real work of guidance, as a participant in the action behind the scenes at that time.

When they were showing me this, profound emotion arose in me—and it can still affect me whenever I tune into it. It explains the deep love I have for the United States (despite all that's gone awry in its direction as a nation since those early days at its inception). It explains the profound hope I still hold for this country—knowing that the signing of the Declaration of Independence was a huge evolutionary step, not only for the newly-emerging group of Americans, but for all of humanity at the time.

Guides Change as Our Lives Change

As time went on, I found myself more simply dialoguing with my guides as a group and not so interested in them as individuals. One thing I learned, however, is that the group wasn't a set entity that continued over time. As my life changed, and as different karma came on board—or different tasks came my way to perform—certain guides left and others arrived. There seems to be a few who have remained throughout, but many have come and gone over the years.

And as I've grown in my ability to hear them clearly and also to attune to my Higher Self, the way they interact with me has also changed. For example, when I was writing my first book, *The Art of*

Letting Go, I had a "book team"—a group of specific guides—who gathered every morning, as I was getting ready to write at my word processor.

The image they showed me of themselves was a group of people getting ready to sit down together at a table for a meeting—getting their coffee first, then settling into chairs and talking with one another. (I doubt this is what was really taking place—but the image exactly fits the feeling I had.)

At any rate, I'd wait until they seemed ready to go. And then I'd be poised to write whatever they "sent" me. The first three chapters came to me word for word—just perfectly. I could hardly type fast enough. I realized it was a word-for-word channeling I was receiving, and I was thrilled—mainly because it was so easy. The words just flowed out of me. Very little editing needed to be done to those first few chapters.

Then the day came when I was poised and ready for the words to come for the fourth chapter. Suddenly a whole idea popped into my head—no words. Confused, I asked what this was. Where were the words? And they answered, "You know well enough how to write; you can figure that part out. We just wanted to get you started with the first few chapters. Now we're just going to give you the ideas to write about in the order to write them."

I was chagrined because coming up with the actual writing was harder than just channeling the words. But I found I could do it. And it continued to be fun to see what ideas they'd come up with for me to write about.

Writing my last book, *Awakening to the Fifth Dimension*, was a different experience. I again had a book team with whom I felt very connected. And I knew they were energetically influencing me in the writing. But the writing this time was coming more from a higher aspect of myself. The words streamed down from within and yet also from above me.

When I asked them about this, they answered that I had matured enough spiritually to be able now to pull the ideas and words from Universal Mind myself. They said they'd be assisting me energetically as I wrote, but they didn't need to be so involved in the ideas and the writing. They did assure me, however, that they would very much be on board when it came time to market the book.

This relieved me, as marketing something I've created has never been my favorite job. It felt good to know they'd be there with me, doing things from the other realms that I couldn't do to get what felt like "our" book out. I wasn't alone with this project.

I just needed to do my part as the one in the physical body to do what they couldn't. This gave me an incredible sense of support—and also a sense of responsibility in both finishing the book and getting it out to people who would benefit from it. I didn't want to let my team down by not performing well in my role in "our" project.

It can be interesting, I think, for all of us who are currently involved in projects to do with Ascension or with assisting humanity or the planet in any way, to tune into the invisible beings who are also participating. We can become a lot more conscious of the spiritual purpose of our projects, and we can also feel more supported in what we're hoping to accomplish.

Love of our Guides

One thing that has impacted me recently is the depth of love I experience that guides appear to have for the people they are serving. Over and over again in the healings I give to people, I am deeply moved by the tender caring in which their guides hold them. And often too I hear guides expressing a sense of honor and privilege they hold for being in that capacity to guide and protect that person.

I realize that, even with all the contact I've had with my own guides over the years, I have never until couple of years ago actually allowed myself to take in the fullness of the love they hold for me. I am aware on a much deeper level than ever before that I have never, ever been alone or unloved in this life. They have always been with me, guiding me through the darkest experiences—and at times energetically cradling me when I have felt the most lost.

And I know this is true for all of us. None of us is alone or lost; our guides are always present. It's just a matter of tuning into the level of vibration at which they exist and experiencing their presence. And if we can't feel them, then this is what we can pray for. In my experience, if this type of prayer is sincere, it is always answered.

Opening to Our Galactic Heritage

Another phenomenon I notice happening for a number of people lately is a remembering of their galactic heritage—a knowing that they originally came from another planet or galaxy.

Some simply have a subtle feeling about this; others are waking up to full memory of other places in the universe where they've existed, or other extraordinary experiences they've had off-planet over a long period of evolution. This used to be the stuff of science fiction or fantasy. Now many grounded and otherwise "ordinary" people are realizing they have not always incarnated on earth.

At one point in my work, many clients who came to me appeared to be Souls who had recently incarnated on the Earth for the first time. They were people who were quite ungrounded and seemed to still be trying to figure out how things operated here. In recognizing them from this perspective, I was able to give them a lot of validation and guidance—as well as a sense of identity from which they could function here more effectively.

Yet I had never really thought much about where I myself might have come from originally. I'd always known I'd been here on Earth since very ancient times, and just assumed I'd come from somewhere "out there", as I believe most—if not all— of us have. And I wasn't much interested in exploring the subject for myself.

Introduction to the Pleiadians

Then one day a couple of years ago, as I described in Chapter 6, I attended a workshop given by Christine Day, a woman who calls herself a "Pleiadian Ambassador". I went there along with some friends kind of as a lark, thinking it might be fun just to learn about the Pleiadians. I was therefore quite surprised to have the profound realization during the workshop that I myself had come from the Pleiades—and that that heritage was very strong in me.

The Pleiadian energy in the workshop was incredibly powerful, and at first I thought I was just being influenced by it and imagining things. But more and more memories and realizations opened up in me throughout the weekend, and I could no longer doubt the reality of what I was remembering.

At one point, I had a most beautiful memory come to me, in which I was in a temple in Atlantis—back before the dark energies started permeating the cultures there. I had just recently "arrived" from visiting my home in the Pleiades for a while, and was part of an order in a temple of some kind. It was night time in my memory, and I was in a large room with tall window openings. The shutters on these windows had been closed, but I suddenly had the urge to open them and look out into the night sky.

As I did this, I was startled to see a space ship coming toward me, and incredible joy burst forth in me. I knew it was my Pleiadian "family" come to visit me and see how I was doing. In my experience of remembering this, I began weeping—both with the joy I was remembering for their arrival, and also with sadness that at this current point in my evolution I hadn't been consciously in touch with this family since those ancient days. It brought a new experiential meaning to the word *family* for me.

In another experience, I was in this same room in a temple—but with a number of other women. There was a part of the roof that had somehow been opened to the night sky, and we were all there with heads uplifted to the sky, chanting the most beautiful chant together that was designed to "call in the ships" to us.

As can be imagined, I was reeling by the time I left the workshop, attempting to connect all this new knowing about myself with the person I'd been before I'd entered the workshop. When I got home, the experiences deepened further, often accompanied by profound sobbing from the joy and recognition of a primary aspect of my identity I'd not been aware of before.

Pleiadian Friends

In one of my meditation experiences a couple of weeks later, two Pleiadian figures became very clear to me. They'd shown up in the workshop and were now speaking to me. The male figure, who identified himself as A-Ram, looked and felt so familiar and dear to me, my heart immediately began aching with love and recognition. He was someone I knew I had grown up with through several lifetimes in the Pleiades—perhaps like a brother—but something much deeper.

I can't describe the depth of joy I experienced in first speaking with him, feeling as if I were finally meeting him again after such a long time. We had been so close, it was almost as if we were a part of each other.

The other Pleiadian, whose name was Sha-Rohn, was female—a gorgeous feminine being, both physically and energetically. She seemed to have beautiful clear colors floating all around her, like scarves blowing in a breeze, and she emanated a most profound, gentle love. She too was familiar, perhaps like a "cousin".

Needless to say, I fell in love with both these beings. They appeared to me every time I meditated—and when I tuned in other times in my daily life, I realized they were there with me then, too.

It was as if they were watching everything I was doing with great interest, wanting to learn what it was like to have a fourth-dimensional body. It was more than just a casual interest—it was as if it was part of a plan for them to now be here with me, that we were going to be doing something together and they needed to know how things function on this plane.

Merging

Then one day A-Ram told me he would like to have the experience of merging with me. I was startled, but then he explained that this was a way in which the Pleiadians "hug" each other—they actually merge molecules with each other. I was very excited about having the opportunity to experience this.

He, on the other hand, seemed just a tad nervous. He explained that this was to be the first time he would be doing this with someone in a fourth-dimensional body, and that he was not sure how he would respond to the density and all the third and fourth-dimensional energies that I was still carrying in my body. But, he said, he'd prepared for it and would like to try it.

I had no idea what to expect—if anything. Was I making this all up? But I said yes, I'd like to try it. Well, I was totally unprepared for what was to take place. As he initiated the process, I could feel his energy (such luscious, clear, loving energy!) enter my body, and I suddenly became aware that our very molecules were indeed mingling with each other.

I could see and feel what I knew to be my own molecules swirling all around his—and the incredible bliss in this experience was unlike any I'd ever experienced before. I felt I'd come "home" in a way I'd never before felt—and a shimmering ecstasy reverberated throughout my whole being.

This probably lasted only about a minute, although it felt much longer. Then he let me know he needed to leave to transmute the lower energies he'd picked up in my body. His departure was kind of abrupt, but I just laughed—knowing that the denseness of my fourth-dimensional body must have been hard for him. But the bliss remained in me for quite a while.

A few days later, Sha-Rohn told me she'd like to have the same experience with me. It was a similar experience for me with her, although her energy was quite different from his, very feminine. She too needed to leave rather quickly afterwards to take what I imagined must be like an "energy shower".

A while later, I became aware that they were with me quite constantly—and that now they were each merged part way inside of me—he on my left side, and she on my right. And that is where they now are, every time I tune into them. It's a sensation that feels so right—as if the three of us are one being. I'm assimilating what they know and experience and I feel this is helping to lighten the density of my body; and they are assimilating what I know and experience in the 4D Earth.

I don't know what all this means—or where it will lead. I just know that it is extremely real and I don't doubt any of it at this point. There are times, in fact, when this other-worldly realm I'm in with them is even more real to me than the physical one is.

Visit from a Blue Being

A young woman I know has felt like a stranger in a strange land ever since she can remember. Life has been extremely challenging for her on almost every front. Recently she told me she'd been reading something about the star system known as "Lyra" and that she suddenly found herself inexplicably weeping with an intense longing to go "home" there to be with her "cosmic family."

She was totally startled by this feeling. She had never even heard of Lyra before; yet here she was yearning to "return" there. As she sat puzzling over this, she heard inwardly that indeed she was originally from this distant galaxy. She began a fervent prayer to be taken there to be introduced to her Lyran family. She had no idea what she was actually praying for or how this might possibly come about. She just knew she had to connect in some way with a family to whom she now understood she belonged.

One night a few weeks later she awakened to find a luminous blue being hovering near her bed, smiling gently and holding out its hand to her. Startled and overcome with excitement in feeling the deep love emanating from this being who seemed strangely familiar to her, she felt herself begin to leave her body.

This was an unbelievable dream come true. And yet suddenly fear shot through her as she felt herself separating from her physical form. And she immediately fell back into her body. The blue being remained a few more moments and then disappeared.

She felt devastated by this experience. Her prayers had been unbelievably answered, and yet she had blown her opportunity to meet a being who felt more familiar to her than any person she'd ever known in her life. She was furious with herself but knew she'd had no control over her fear. She wondered dejectedly if she'd ever have another opportunity to connect with her blue being family again.

My guess is that she will. Her response of fear at the prospect of leaving her physical body is a common one for those who have never had out-of-body experiences before. The next time she has that opportunity, she can hopefully be more aware and intentional in staying calm and trusting.

And until she has this opportunity, she at least has had the experience of seeing and energetically connecting with a being with whom she felt to be part of her "true" family.

I believe all of us moving rapidly through our Ascension process may begin to remember more about our galactic heritage at some point. I believe that many of us sometimes visit our "homelands" at night in the sleep state and bring back both a feeling of bliss and homesickness when we awaken in the morning. I'm finding in my work that many of us have guides from those faraway places.

Star Seeds

Even though it's likely we have all originally come from somewhere else in the universe, I've found that certain people I've known and worked with have evidently come from very distant galaxies—and some quite recently, as well.

As I've noted, these people often find the human form very difficult to get used to, both psychologically and physically, even after many years in this incarnation. Some I've worked with have actually had doctors tell them their brains or their nervous systems are different from the norm. Usual medical procedures and therapies simply don't work on them.

The best success they have for treatment is with modalities of energy healing, although even those sometimes do not work. Some of them even have bodies that create interference with technology in their environments. Friends sometimes jokingly throw around the notion that they are "ETs". Little do they know how accurate they may be.

One thing about these people attuned to distant galaxies, however, is they seem to be strikingly clear they are here for humanity's transition. They feel they've been summoned to Earth to do a specific job that perhaps "ordinary" humans are not able to do. Many of these people identify themselves as "star seeds", and their soul missions generally show up relatively early in their lives.

Working with the
Archangels & Ascended Masters

It seems common for many of us consciously moving through Ascension to be in contact with both Archangels and Ascended Masters. These beings do indeed seem to be increasingly available to all of us when we call them in for help or guidance.

The Archangels, in particular, have been familiar to me most of my life. As a young child, I began sensing the presence of angels around me. As an adult, from time to time I've delved into reading about them and attempted to communicate with them, with varying degrees of success.

But in the last couple of years I've had more kinesthetic experiences with them. I now often feel them with me, mostly during meditation. At times I can actually feel them in my aura—and even inside my body—when I experience them working on rewiring my brain or my body. There's an incredible gentleness with these ministrations, as well as a power and clarity that feels different from the touch of any other beings I've ever experienced. They definitely are a species different from human beings.

But what really cracked me up at one point is when I first called the Archangels in before a difficult dental appointment. As I was sitting in the chair awaiting the dentist, I called them in—and suddenly I was very aware that Metatron was present. (I can't say exactly how I knew it was he, but I did—it's just that they all seem to have a particular energetic signature—as I sense we all do. And I simply knew it was Metatron.)

Interestingly, the main vibration I picked up from him was one of curiosity. It was as if he was there looking around, picking up instruments and studying them, very interested in all the technology and gadgets. He also had someone with him who had been a dentist when he'd been incarnated, and this man was explaining things to him. I just chuckled at the whole experience.

When the dentist came in and began to work on me, I was aware that all three of them were involved in the procedure. I could feel them all gazing down on me, making sure all was going well. Metatron was both holding energy for the procedure and eagerly learning the practical, physical details of it as well.

I'm not sure what brought my conversation with my dentist around to it, but he suddenly told me he always says a prayer before doing his work to Apollonia, the saint who guides dentists. I smiled and offered, "Well, I call in the Archangels—so I guess we're in really good company!"

Since that first dentist appointment with Metatron, I have called him in on every other one I've had and he always appears. For this reason, my dentist appointments are a lot less aggravating than they had been before his entrance into them.

The Ascended Masters have always felt quite different to me from the angels. Having been incarnated on Earth as human beings, they hold a more similar energy to ours, and perhaps they understand certain things happening here more clearly than the Archangels for this reason.

There are certain Ascended Masters we all tend to relate to more than others, perhaps because we've known them during one of their periods of incarnation. For me, St. Germaine has always felt very familiar, perhaps due to my times with him during the American Revolution. Yeshua and Sanat Kumara are especially familiar, as well.

Recently I also feel a desire to connect with three of the female Ascended Masters: Mother Mary, Anna (Jesus's grandmother), and Mary Magdalene. There is something very comforting about the presence of this holy trio, as they seem to have a special understanding of what the emotional experience of living on Earth is for many of us.

It's important, I believe, to remember that the help and guidance of all Ascended Masters and Archangels are available to us during these times of Ascension. I find that the more we can remember to ask for their help and to trust we're receiving it, the more we can be aware of their presence and the more clear our communication with them becomes.

We Are All Magnificent Beings

Sometimes the opening into other dimensions of existence includes experiences of *ourselves* as beings in these other dimensions. I had one of these experiences a couple of years ago.

Over the years I had read and heard from numerous sources about how we human beings are so much more than we think we are—that we are, in actuality, magnificent, complex beings with powers far beyond what we can imagine. I'd always believed this and to some extent felt that I'd experientially grasped this truth.

I understood we use only a very small percentage of our brain and our DNA—and figured there must be some use for the rest of our brains and the DNA we hadn't tapped into yet. I had also experienced profound spiritual dimensions within myself that extend far beyond my body and mind, and I'd understood that these dimensions exist within all of us.

But, until a particular night a few years ago, I had not directly experienced what is meant by the concept that we human beings are actually "magnificent" beings. I hadn't fully grasped the magnitude or the profundity of this reality. It was still an intellectual understanding.

Heart Opening Experience

But as I was sitting quietly reading one night, I was about to experience this reality on a direct and conscious level. I became aware rather suddenly of a deep, quiet movement happening in my chest. This was a familiar sensation—I always know something is happening with my heart when this happens, that a new opening is about to occur—so I paid close attention.

It's a somewhat uncomfortable feeling initially, as if my heart is being pulled open against some inherent resistance I have. Yet it is one of the most profoundly pleasant sensations, as well. And as always, tears began flowing, as I moved with the energy of opening to this space within me.

As I felt this energy beginning to move freely through my chest, I became aware of myself as a being that was quite a bit larger than my physical being, maybe 10 feet tall—and I was, well...magnificent. This is the only word that kept coming to me, although it is woefully inadequate to describe what I was experiencing.

I was aware of many multidimensional layers of myself, all flowing in tiny universes of their own and all concurrently with each other. There was an immense lightness about my self—almost as if I were translucent and airy, filled with light and brilliant colors.

I was also aware that I possessed great power—far beyond what we talk about in our third-and fourth-dimensional human state about "creating our own reality". This power included the ability to create much more than my own personal reality.

And the love that was present in this experience! It pervaded everything and was everywhere around and within me, powerful and all-embracing. It was clear that this is what drives all of existence on this level of reality—wherever I was in that moment.

I became aware that I was with other vast beings like myself in this experience. We weren't doing anything in particular together—just casually hanging out and communicating. But it suddenly came very clear to me that all of us—every single human being on this planet—is a magnificent, multidimensional being just as I knew myself to be at that moment. We are simply not aware of it.

We Are So Much More Than We Think We Are

And with this realization I found myself sobbing, feeling a profound grief for the whole human race, for what we have been through for so many thousands of years. It was poignantly clear that our current experience of who we think we are is so limited, so constrained, so small and weak. Our little human bodies and minds—even with as much spiritual awareness as many of us have attained—are such a tiny part of who we all actually are.

I had been aware of what many sources tell us about how we on Earth were once fully aware of our spiritual splendor, our direct connection to Source, and our immense powers in many dimensions of our being. And how, through the Fall of Consciousness, we all fell into a total experience of separation from what we once knew ourselves to be—into a dark, dense state of consciousness living in duality and immense suffering. And how, for thousands of years, we have been locked into this tremendously limited state of awareness known as the Third Dimension.

But this sadness was soon replaced by enormous waves of joy as I realized that this forgetfulness and feeling of being lost in a dense and limited world of duality was now coming to an end.

We Are Re-Awakening

I knew—and continue to know, even now that the poignancy of that experience has dissipated some with time—that we are indeed in profound times of transformation. Awakening is occurring for so many of us on the planet, at a speed that could almost be alarming if it weren't so exciting. Of course, the correct term would be *re-awakening*, for it is a matter of *remembering* who we actually are, not waking up for the first time.

But it's not a return to another time in our history, either. We are not regressing. We are moving ahead, leaping very quickly into a higher level of evolution. We are re-awakening to what we once knew, but we've now gained the experience of what it is to be caught in darkness and suffering for thousands of years. This has provided us with a wisdom we have attained the hard way—but we have attained it.

We've learned that with the gift of free will, we are capable of shutting ourselves down, forgetting who we are, forgetting our connection to Source—forgetting that we are, in actuality, God. And it is likely that we will never forget this profoundly difficult learning.

The Veils are Thinning

I've been very fortunate to be as attuned to beings on other realms as I have been over the years—and especially since Ascension has really set in recently. But I believe that many of us, especially those of us who are Ascension lightworkers, have always been in touch with our guides and beings from other realms.

Many simply are not aware of it—or have not made it important to be aware of it. They've simply acted on inner guidance without thinking much about the specifics of how they were receiving it.

What I think is important during these times, however, is to notice how much easier it is now since we've entered the Fourth Dimension, to be aware of other realities that other beings live in and to be in touch with those who are wanting to communicate with us.

The veils are getting thinner, and communication through the veils is easier. We are losing our density and are closer in vibration to our guides and other celestial beings than ever before. I believe it's time for us to consciously rejoin them at long last.

Chapter 11

Miracles Abounding

I'm observing an increasing number of events I would call "miracles" happening in both my own life and in that of people around me these days. Sometimes we simply don't notice them. At other times we do see them, but they show up so often now that they become almost commonplace to us as we move through the Fourth Dimension. They're events and situations that in the past I would have exclaimed over with great delight, but now just nod my head to with a smile.

This is especially so regarding what we might identify as wonderful and unexpected experiences that seem miraculous but which we realize we've helped to create through strong intention and keeping our vibration high. We can see with these experiences that we've been successful in manifesting something we've wanted in our lives.

We might also use the word "miracle" to describe a dramatic and positive change in ourselves that's happened within a short period of time. Or an event that appears to be perfectly orchestrated to bring about a desired outcome.

These types of miracles are often events filled with synchronicities. They also demonstrate to us the power of Grace, yet we can also observe our own participation in them. In my own experience, I identify them as "high fourth-dimensional miracles".

There is another type of miracle that seems to occur less frequently. This is an event for which we cannot determine any causality. It seems to happen out of the blue, completely as Grace. Nor does there appear to be any agency involved in this occurrence: we have played no obvious, direct role in causing it. These I identify as "fifth-dimensional miracles".

These wondrous miracles have happened throughout history. We can read about them in sources such as the Bible and the ancient Hindu Veda texts. The fact that they've happened down through the ages in which humanity was locked in the Third Dimension may be why they have the impact on us they do when they occur: they demonstrate so clearly that even if we're still functioning in 3D or 4D consciousness, this type of 5D event can happen in our lives. In 3D and 4D consciousness we can't understand how these types of miracles occur—or even why. We only know they occasionally do and they serve, in part, to give us a vision, a preview of what is to come in our 5D lives.

Miracles are a reminder of the higher dimensions we will inhabit at some point in our evolution. And if we keep our minds open, we can expect more and more of them to occur as we find our way into the Fifth Dimension.

Many of us can point to at least one miracle that's happened in our life. I've actually experienced a few of them, but none so powerful as those that have happened in the past fifteen years since I've been aware of the Ascension process.

Miracle Healing

During the early 2000s, I made a trip to Brazil to see the healer known as John of God. I went because I was at my wit's end in trying to get well from a very debilitating case of fibromyalgia. I had felt powerfully drawn to see him, despite some doubts I had about those known as "miracle healers".

But as soon as I stepped onto the property known as the "Casa", where he gave his healings, I felt the magical energy there. I knew something very different happened in this place, something out of the ordinary. And the energy that enveloped me was deeply infused with love. My heart opened wide, and I was ready to experience whatever that place had to offer me.

What I discovered there was what I can only call "Harry Potter energy". It was a culture all its own, run through with tales of miracles, strange rules of conduct and healing prescriptions that would make you laugh until you started seeing how they actually worked.

For me, there were many small magical things that occurred, and numerous beautiful and profound experiences. Some involved the healing beings there in the invisible realms, and some involved the people who worked there. But perhaps the biggest miracle that happened for me was a particular physical healing I experienced.

At one point, a group of about 30 of us were directed to come to a room at a given time and sit down on the benches there. We were about to receive "psychic surgery". We were instructed to close our eyes and to hold our hand over the part of our body we wanted healed (and if there were more places than one, to just hold it over our heart). We were told that John would shortly come into the room and do the healing.

About 30 seconds later, he told us our healing was complete. What?! John had come in and done it that quickly? And we were supposed to believe we were healed? I had a lot of faith in these processes by now, but this was challenging. As we were filing out of the room, we were told that we needed to get back immediately to our rooms, lie down in bed—and stay there for 24 hours, so we could fully accept the healing into our bodies.

I heard the warning in this and half-believed that something might begin shortly that I needed to be in bed for—but I was hungry. I was smelling the "healing soup" they served every day, and so I decided I'd eat the soup before heading back to the motel where I was staying.

Well, I ate about two spoonfuls, when suddenly a bolt of energy coursed through my body and I thought I was going to pass out. My face almost fell into the bowl of soup. I immediately awkwardly gathered my things and stumbled out toward the taxi stand to find a ride back to my motel. I barely made it to my bed before I passed out for a number of hours.

By the end of the 24 hours, much of which I had spent sleeping, I felt great—but I had no idea if any miracle of healing had happened for me. I just shrugged and continued on with the program there, not thinking much about it—just trusting that something must have happened to some part of my body I wasn't aware of yet.

Without going into detail about the biggest physical issue I'd been dealing with during my illness—severe constipation—a day after the end of that 24 hour period, I suddenly had a huge surprise when I had my first natural bowel movement in over a year. And from that point on, it was as if I'd never been dealing with that problem at all.

My father had died of colon cancer, and I had been convinced I was probably on my way down that same road, when this miracle happened. Although my colon has continued to be a vulnerable part of my body and at times has given me problems if I'm not careful, the situation like I'd had before the healing has never revisited me again.

At the time, I saw it as a total miracle. Something beyond my comprehension had taken place. Today, after a number of other similar experiences in my life—and in others' experiences I've witnessed—this is something I now feel to be familiar and even expected.

We live in a quantum field in which all things are possible. We are no longer restricted to third-dimensional possibilities that are governed by rigid rules and restrictions. As we move closer and closer to fifth-dimensional consciousness, the extraordinary will become more and more ordinary.

Miracle Communication

A few years later, as I previously described, I found myself in India at the Oneness University taking a 21-day course, along with about 200 people from around the world, to learn how to give the Oneness Blessing, otherwise known as *deeksha*. This was another place that felt Harry Potterish to me—or a place in which fifth-dimensional events and experiences seemed to be commonplace.

One experience that stands out for me occurred when those giving the training announced that we would be visited that evening by several of the people connected to the university who had committed themselves to 24-hour-a-day meditation on world peace. Just the fact that there existed such people was striking to me. But seeing and then meeting one of them up close was a truly extraordinary experience.

The three meditators entered the hall in slow motion. They were all dressed in white, wrapped in great swaths of white cloth, almost zombie-like—and they walked up the aisle in a dream-like state. We were told this was because they were in the state of delta (usually known as the sleep state), the level of consciousness they stayed conscious in for days and days at a time. It was a marvel they could walk and interact with people at all.

At any rate, they were led up onto the stage, and we all lined up so we could each interact for a couple of minutes with one of them. I had no idea what to expect. I thought I might peer into the person's eyes for a bit and maybe feel an exchange of energy of some kind.

I was taken to stand in front of a lovely looking young woman whose eyes revealed such profound depths, I was immediately stunned. After about five seconds of looking into my eyes, she suddenly started laughing. Truly and fully laughing, with her head thrown back. I had no idea what she was laughing about; but of course, I caught the laughing bug, and I started laughing, as well.

And then we couldn't stop. From time to time, she'd grab me and hug me—but then she'd start laughing again. We both had tears streaming down our faces by the time one of the facilitators finally took me by the shoulders and led me away, so others could have their turn.

By that point, I couldn't stop laughing. I was laughing so hard, in fact, that I couldn't stand or walk on my own to the back of the hall where I was supposed to go to lie down on the floor. The person leading me was actually dragging me there, because my knees had given out.

And meanwhile, as might be expected, everyone all around me had broken out laughing. It was clear I was simply laughing out of a mindless, natural joy that sprang from the depths of my being, and no one could resist it.

When I finally found a place on the floor in the back, I continued to have spasms of laughter. But soon I began thinking that maybe I was disturbing people who wanted to be silent, so I decided to get up and go outside into the cool night air. It was glorious! As I walked around, I continued to burst out laughing everywhere I walked—over nothing at all. Just pure glee.

Suddenly ravenous, I eventually found my way to the dining hall, where many were eating in devotional silence as we'd been instructed to. I had a thought that maybe I shouldn't disturb them; but then I went in anyway, bringing raucous laughter with me. I loaded my plate with the food they offered us—food that was truly bland and tasteless. (They evidently thought that Westerners couldn't take any the spices they usually used, so they left them all out.) I then sat down with a number of others around me at the table.

Much to my surprise and delight, the taste of the food was miraculously wonderful to me. I began groaning with pleasure as I piled it in, exclaiming joyfully how delicious it was. And laughter broke out at my table and all around me, simply because of my strange enjoyment of this food that we all knew to be almost tasteless. And soon I had the whole room laughing with me.

After that I found my way to my dormitory bed, and of course had everyone in the room there laughing with me about every little thing. I seemed to be infecting all I encountered with uncontrollable laughter. It took a while that night, but I finally found my way into sleep.

In the morning my laughter had subsided, but a quiet and profound joy enveloped me. Before the day in the hall began, I went to the room where they had computers, as I needed to see if a particular email had come for me from someone I was planning to meet in India, right after the workshop ended.

To my surprise I saw there was an email from someone back home—someone I had just recently met before I'd left. I was wondering why she would write me an email, when I knew she knew we needed to be in silence during this workshop and not get involved in things back home. I almost didn't open the email. But then something prompted me to.

The woman writing me was a hands-on healer I didn't know well or feel any particular connection to at that point, so her email had an especially powerful impact on me. She told me about an experience she had just had the day before (which would have been my previous evening).

She told me that she had been about to start a healing on a man when, out of nowhere, I "appeared" to her in the room, and that I was laughing with incredible joy. She was so startled by this and felt such powerful energy with it, that she fell to her knees on the floor and began sobbing with joy. She had no idea how she could be seeing me there in the room.

When she finally got up a while later, the man on her table had tears in his eyes. He said he'd just had a powerful healing, not knowing what had happened. He didn't know anything about what she had experienced. And, of course, neither of them knew what I was experiencing, probably at about the same time.

Nor did I know I had "appeared" somewhere else. So of course, this says a whole lot about this woman. The fact that she could have been aware of me and what I was experiencing half-way across the world was extraordinary. And she was, and is, I was to find out, a powerful intuitive healer and seer.

But the true miracle, I believe, was in the divine orchestration that later became apparent when I returned home. This woman, because of her experience with me, turned out to be extremely instrumental in setting me up to give *deeksha* eventually to hundreds of people in the area over the next couple of years.

Our connection through the quantum field seemed miraculous at the time; but as with my experience with John of God, it soon became an event that felt almost ordinary and to be expected in the times we were now living.

Miracle on Mt. Shasta

There are probably a lot of people who have experienced miracles on Mt. Shasta—it just seems to be a magical place where out of the ordinary events happen. Mine was rather minor, but an extremely important one for me.

It took place during a workshop I was taking with Dell Morris, learning how to perform Quantum Healing. One ailment that had not been healed in my trips to Brazil with John of God was a serious sleeping disorder. My insomnia had become so bad that I needed to take powerful narcotics by that time, just to knock myself out at night.

I was experiencing terrible side effects from the drugs, but my fear of going off them was intense. The thought of having to live through sleeplessness again, night after night, paralyzed me. And I also knew that trying to go off narcotics could be extremely hard on me, as well.

But I was determined. So one night after a healing I'd received specifically on the sleeping disorder, I went to bed without having taken any drugs. I was fully prepared to spend an entire night staring at the ceiling, as I'd done on countless nights before I'd started taking the drugs to sleep. But I wanted to show myself I had faith in the healings. I had had small miracles happen from the healings by this point, but this was a big one that I wasn't at all sure I could trust.

Well, I not only fell asleep that night—I awoke the next morning feeling the most refreshed I had in years. The miracle had happened. I threw out all my drugs and had no trouble at all with withdrawal.

This was to be an especially important miracle for me, as it convinced me entirely about the reality of long-distance healing. And it was something I could learn to do myself and give to others. I was excited that I no longer would have to travel to Brazil or anywhere else to receive this kind of healing.

It was finally clear to me that the quantum field was everywhere and healing could take place anywhere on the planet, simply through thought and intention. Since then I have experienced and witnessed numerous miraculous healings both physical and emotional, for people I've given healings to.

Miracle Manifestation

Over the years I have practiced and taught a number of different methods of manifestation and have had varying degrees of success with them. At times I've enjoyed delightful, magical results. And at others, it seems that nothing happens.

What I've learned is that manifestation doesn't happen solely through a particular method we use—even if we do it on a daily basis. It takes consistent awareness of our thoughts, emotions, and intentions, and bringing unconscious patterns and desires to the surface.

There are times it takes a lot of work to come into complete coherence with whatever it is we're wanting to manifest. And sometimes what we're trying to manifest just isn't in alignment with our highest good—or it's not right timing for it. So the universe doesn't respond as we'd hoped.

Realizing all this after a while, I finally dropped all attempts at manifesting what I thought I wanted or needed. I instead shifted into a consciousness of simply allowing and accepting whatever came forward in my life—and welcoming it. This was a beautiful approach, I found—much more relaxing. There was a feeling of trust in the Divine and an attitude of deep surrender that brought me a great deal of peace.

A New Manifestation Process

And so it was with some surprise last year to find myself responding to a suggestion in a guided meditation I was listening to, to manifest something I wanted to have happen in my life. I was about to skip the suggestion, when I inwardly heard a strong directive to follow the instructions and see what would happen. After some reluctance, I gave in and asked what I should try to manifest. At once, the idea popped into my mind to manifest the book I had just begun to write.

I had been feeling an inner urgency to write this book, but I'd had experiences in the past in publishing a book that fed a belief that the process could take a long time—and that it could be difficult getting everything done that was needed along the way. So I hadn't moved fully into thinking about the publication of what I was beginning to write.

But I was drawn to trying what the meditation was suggesting. In following its instructions, I decided I wanted to create ease in writing the book and in getting it edited and published—and also as quickly as possible. The next instruction was to allow a date to come to me by which time I wanted the manifestation to take place.

This was a somewhat new approach, and I liked it. In the past, I had generally chosen a date (if I came up with one at all) through my rational mind or desire. Allowing the date to come to me, instead of deciding on one in my mind, felt good.

And suddenly I heard "the first of June". I immediately reacted with, "Oh that's much too soon—I can't possibly have it all done in just three months' time!" It was the very end of February at this point. But that date is what I just kept hearing, as I also kept seeing the image of myself in my living room holding my book in my hand on June 1. So that's what I decided—on June 1, I would be holding my book in my hand.

Then the next instruction in the exercise was to break down all the elements of what needed to happen for my final manifestation to come into being and allow dates to come to me for when those elements would be completed. I gulped with uncertainty. First I'd have to finish writing the book. I knew it wasn't going to be lengthy—but still, there wasn't much time to actually take time to write. I was busy working on other things during the day—I basically had time to write only at night and on weekends.

And yet I heard "By April 1". In other words, I'd have essentially one month to complete the writing of the book. Okay. I was game. I would work on it in all my free time. I declared I'd finish writing by April 1.

The next thing that was needed was finding an editor (and finding the money to pay him or her). And then the editing needed to be finished. I heard "By May 1". Yikes—one month to do all that? No way. But I was well into this by now. So I said, Okay, it will be edited and ready for publishing by May 1.

Then the last step came to me: I needed to find a self-publishing company that I could afford, as well as one that I could trust. I had not had a good experience with a traditional publishing company with my previous book, so I knew I wanted to self-publish this time.

But I also knew there were a great number of self-publishing houses out there and that some writers I knew had been badly cheated by ones they'd connected with. I knew I'd have to do a large amount of research to find one that was going to work for me.

So all this, plus the time for them to actually publish the book— could it all possibly be done in the final month before I was to be holding the book in my hand? Again my belief was really being tested. But I simply decided to go for it. Every step came to me with such clarity and firmness, that I just decided to trust it.

But then, like with so many inner experiences I have—and some of them really powerful—a couple of days later, I'd strangely forgotten all about the process I'd done and the intentions I'd set.

The Steps of the Miracle Unfold

But I was into the writing—and still feeling the gentle but persistent urgency to get the book written. I was up late every night and worked through every weekend of March. And meanwhile, a friend of mine who'd been a professional editor volunteered to edit my book when it was ready, and to simply accept a percentage of the royalties for her services. An incredible boon! But even with this, I wasn't remembering the manifestation process I'd done.

Then one night I finally came to the end of my own editing of what I'd written and decided it was time to hand it all over to her the next day. I was on my computer and I glanced down to see what time it was—and I suddenly saw the date: March 31. And then I remembered! This was the date that had come to me to be finished with the writing.

I was amazed, unbelieving. I thought, "Well, this is probably just coincidence. It's neat, but I really have no control now over the editing process. I have no idea how long she'll take with each chapter, or what other things she's got planned to do this month. And I don't want to rush her—she's doing me such a favor." And I just let the whole thing go, deciding to accept whatever might happen. And again, I forgot about the manifestation process I'd done.

But then the end of April was drawing close, and I remembered the schedule I'd agreed to. My friend had done a lot of the editing, but had not yet finished the last few chapters. It was around April 27 when she told me that she was going away for a week or so and would get to the last chapters when she got back. I had to admit I was disappointed. I was really hoping for the magic to happen. But I just let it go, reminding myself how fortunate I was to have the editing done so quickly.

Then on April 30—you've probably guessed it—my friend called to tell me she'd decided to just finish the last few chapters before she left town. They were completed if I wanted to pick them up. I smiled with delight. Maybe it was all going to work as I'd seen it, after all!

Now I was into May, knowing I had to find a publishing company, find the money to pay it, and then let go of the whole thing—because I had no idea how long it might take to actually publish a book. After hours and hours of researching publishing companies online, a number of times I thought I'd finally found one that would work—only to find another site informing me of author boycotts or lawsuits pending against the company I'd chosen.

But then, almost two weeks into May, I finally found one with which I thought I could work. I gave up thinking at this point the book could be published by the end of May. But I was okay with this; I was at least in the last part of the process and amazed at how quickly it had all happened.

So I submitted my manuscript to the publisher. I thought I might get the galleys, if I was lucky, in a week's time. Well, the next day, the text was waiting for me in formatted book form on my computer. Amazing!

Onto the next step: the cover. I figured that would surely have to take some time. It was going to be a custom cover—a photo would have to be found, it would have to be formatted, etc. No problem—again, overnight it was complete—and I liked it! Again I was amazed.

Then the actual book production needed to happen. We were at the end of May at this point, and moving into the Memorial Day weekend. The company told me that the book would be available in a week or so on Amazon. They added that they'd do their best to send the 25 books I'd ordered as soon as possible, but this probably wouldn't happen until the middle of June.

Well, I totally let go of my hopes of a miracle by then. What could I do? I reluctantly released that very clear image I'd had of myself in my living room, holding the book in my hand on June 1—and just accepted reality as it was.

Then, on May 31, I got a call from my editor friend, who had ordered the book online the week before. She told me she'd just received the book. Did I want to see it? It was strange, but I just said "Thanks, but no—I'll be getting my own books soon. No need to bother coming over." Then I suddenly realized what the date was. And I said, "Wait—yes! Bring it over tomorrow!"

And she did. And there I was, standing in my living room, holding my book on June 1. It was small and blue and beautiful, just as I'd seen it in my original vision.

To Control or Not Control?

This whole experience, of course, shifted my attitude toward manifestation. Here I was back to where I was before I'd decided to just let go of trying to control my life by trying to bring in what I wanted, and just allowing life to be as it was. I now knew beyond a doubt that I could successfully bring something seemingly impossible into my life—and in unbelievable timing.

And yet I knew there was also value in the other approach of simply allowing and welcoming everything that came into my life. I was at a cross-roads. Did I want to try to be "in control" of my life again—stepping up and taking charge of what I was manifesting?

I knew that where I was heading—toward fifth-dimensional consciousness—dictated that I needed to do this. I needed to move into that higher, more powerful part of me that could be in charge and direct my life where it needed to go. But in the process of operating from that place in me, would I lose the sense of quiet surrender, acceptance and peace I'd lived in when I had dropped all notions of trying to control my life?

What I've found is a middle path between these two approaches. One of the keys lies in the way in which I came up with both the idea for what to manifest and the dates by which each step would happen. Instead of deciding these things through my rational mind as I would have in the past—I simply allowed them to come to me. I allowed my higher consciousness to tell me what it wanted me to manifest and when everything would be accomplished.

And this is why I'm certain it all worked out as it did. The book was something that "wanted to happen"—and I was willing to be in on the process of bringing it into manifestation. And even though I was on and off in my belief in the process, I had nonetheless declared at the beginning my intention to manifest it in the way I'd heard it wanted to manifest. And this somehow was enough to make it all work. My full heart and a deep sense of clarity had been involved in my intention.

Since that experience, I've been feeling more and more the wonderful sense of surrender and acceptance of whatever wants to unfold in my life. *And* I am very alert to whatever urgings occur within me to create, manifest or do something.

I can say I am feeling more and more at one with my higher consciousness, that part of me that is—and always has been—in charge of my life. I'm feeling less and less any division between who I am and that higher aspect of my being.

Miracle Consciousness

It's important, I believe, if we want to attract miracles into our lives, to shift into the consciousness that not only accepts they can happen, but one that even expects them to.

Yet paradoxically, it may also be important to begin noticing and acknowledging the small miracles that happen in our everyday lives. And to feel the wonder and mystery of them.

It's a cliche to mention the "miracle" people often note when watching a young child grow and learn how to speak and walk— and yet what a miracle that is! Even watching a seed break open and begin to grow into a living plant is a miracle to behold.

And how about the miracle of life, itself? How does life even exist? Taking time to ponder these mysteries can help us to shift past the usual limited, confined territory of the rational mind into those realms beyond, of open possibility, from which miracles emerge.

Chapter 12

Recognizing Fifth-Dimensional Consciousness

The reality structure (or "operating system") we're now all living in is the Fourth Dimension. However, we're not all automatically living from fourth-dimensional consciousness at this point. It's still possible to be functioning from a third-dimensional consciousness, out of habit. Most people on the planet are still doing this.

The good news is that, in understanding what is now available to us, it's possible to begin living from a fourth-dimensional consciousness—or even from a fifth-dimensional consciousness and higher.

By now, I think most of us on a conscious path of Ascension have experienced moments—or even expanded periods of time—of what we might call "fifth-dimensional consciousness" in our daily lives.

We might each describe these experiences somewhat differently. I have described in various ways what they are for me throughout this book; but in general, I would say these experiences are when I feel spacious and light, living in a state of being that is free of all fears, sense of unworthiness, negative emotions, and limitations.

Whatever our version of these experiences may be, we might all say they usually bring us a feeling of joy and a sense of profound freedom and peace. But for most of us, these experiences eventually seem to fade. And it can be easy to fall into depression or even despair when this happens. We can feel a deep sense of loss and wonder what we did wrong to "lose" these experiences.

I've found that it's important to not give way to this kind of reaction when our experiences dissipate. They can be seen instead as "previews" into the state of being we are moving toward in our

Ascension process, and that they're given to us to help keep us moving along in the right direction.

Also, if we look closely, we can see there is still something very essential that has not been lost within us that the experiences have given us: a deep knowing of our true nature and the possibility of being able to maintain that state of consciousness more and more as time goes on.

It's been my experience, as well, that if we keep focused on the state of consciousness we've experienced and explore the different aspects of it, we may realize that we are still experiencing at least some of those aspects in our on-going lives.

And further, I have found that focusing on these experiences of 5D consciousness in a neutral way can also help bring about more of them into our lives.

Common Aspects of Fifth-Dimensional Consciousness

Although each one of us is having our own unique 5D experiences, I believe there are common aspects to many of our experiences. I therefore offer a list of common aspects I have found in those experiences I have had that may spark some recognition of the experiences you may be having.

Trust in the Benevolence of the Universe

For me, in fifth-dimensional consciousness there is a feeling and knowing about the true benevolent nature of the Universe—and life—that is very different from the feeling I have usually had this whole lifetime in the Third Dimension.

Until I began having a number of fifth-dimensional experiences, the world had never felt totally safe or welcoming to me. There had always been some fear about survival, both physical and financial, that I had felt on a subconscious level. There was also a sense of separation and aloneness that had plagued my awareness, no matter how many spiritual "reprogrammings" I'd done or close relationships I'd experienced, attempting to turn this around.

When I'm in fifth-dimensional consciousness, all that is absent. There's a simple trust in life, a knowing that of course my needs will be met. There's no anxiety, no fear. The Universe, the world, life itself, feels friendly and welcoming. I feel precious and important in the unique contributions I offer to the world.

Openness to the "Impossible" Happening

When I find myself stuck in third-dimensional consciousness, I feel caught in the limitations of what my rational mind thinks is possible, based on experiences from the past. There is no sense of my being able to get around the limitations I think I know to be true. And there's often a voice telling me to be "realistic" and not fall into magical thinking.

At times, there's some wisdom in paying attention to that voice: I've found it's possible to simply sail ahead, trusting that things will work out based on blind trust—when not everything is yet set up for things to work out smoothly and in right timing. There's some discernment necessary. There must be trust, yes; but there are also other things that need to be in place, such as being truly attuned to what my higher guidance is telling me, being centered in my Heart, and having a clear intention.

When all this is in place, I can feel myself shifting into a higher consciousness in which I truly understand that what might sound impossible to my third-dimensional mind is actually very possible. I understand that there are no limitations to what I can create. And I can embody the power I know I inherently have to bring about creations I am inwardly directed to manifest.

Heart Expansion

A really common aspect of fifth-dimensional consciousness for all of us, I believe, is a sensation of expansion and openness in the heart—and an outpouring of love from our whole being.

For me, there's a feeling of warmth and emotional receptivity and a flowing of love toward all I encounter and for all of life, including myself. There's a field of love I can feel around me, along with a total absence of judgment or separation. A graciousness moves through me, making way for a deep desire to be of service. And I know this to be my natural state of being, that being in a state of love is what is innately true about me.

There is another aspect of this heart opening experience that is important to note, as well. The emotional love of the heart is only one element involved: there is also an aspect of power in the love that is available to me. I find it's possible to become aware of this higher nature of love—to realize it's a force, a power, a propellant, that can create and change reality. It is indeed the basic inherent nature of all that exists.

Living in the Present Moment

In fifth-dimensional consciousness, I find myself living completely in the present moment—not just in present time, which might include an awareness of what's happening through many hours in a day—but actually in the moment itself. All thoughts of past and future are irrelevant, simply absent. It's a very comfortable zone in which to function.

Once in a while when I'm immersed in the present moment, I'll suddenly remember an appointment or something else I have scheduled in the future and feel anxious that I've lost track of time. But then, if I watch closely, I can see that without fail, I am always somehow reminded exactly when I need to be reminded of that scheduled event.

I am rarely too early or late when I function in this present moment zone. By the clock I might be to some extent. But as for being right on time for the circumstance I'm in, it's always just about right for both myself and for the other people involved in a meeting or appointment with me. There can be a sense of magic that happens with this and curious synchronicities, all telling me I'm on track.

There's also a sense of flow I can actually feel in my body. My body has always been very familiar with living in the moment—it's all it knows. It's just been my mind that has created, or agreed to, the third-dimensional dictates of linear time.

Joy, Peace, Contentment

The basic feeling that permeates my fifth-dimensional experiences is one of joy, peace and deep contentment. It's as if negative emotions don't even exist. It's not as if the feeling of joy is keeping depression at bay; any idea of depression simply isn't in my awareness.

There's an easy acceptance of what-is—no longing, no desire for anything to be different. The constant niggling of unrest and dissatisfaction that has always been present in my third-dimensional consciousness is gone. There's an ease, a comfort, a quiet joy. Whatever is happening in my life is fine. And there's a curiosity about whatever may be next—even an anticipation, knowing it will likely be interesting and engaging.

Full-On Experiences of 5D Consciousness

When I'm functioning in 5D, it's not just me that feels different—the actual world around me feels changed, too. I'm not actually in a different place; I can still see all the same objects and people around me. But they are all vibrating with life in a way I wasn't aware of before when I saw them through 3D eyes. It's almost as if all the cells in everything are dancing.

And strangely enough, there's also a sense that everything I see is happy—even objects: trees, doors, tables, my printer. Needless to say, I myself am charged with happiness. I find myself smiling broadly at everyone I meet, feeling warm and friendly, wanting to engage with them. A palpable love simultaneously envelopes me and pours from me.

There's also a sensation of lightness—a kind of emptiness or lack of density. Everything inside me feels clear and free. There are no issues of self-doubt or self-worth present. These concepts are irrelevant—they don't exist. Nor are there memories or thoughts present about the future. There's just a sense of being.

There appears to be no separation between anyone or anything and myself. I'm empty and clear. And yet I'm also very full—of love, of light, of joy. There is no sense of the small egoic self present. There is nothing of "me" left—just pure consciousness.

Yet at the same time, there is a feeling of being very expanded. I know myself to be a multi-dimensional being—large and spacious—in touch with realities from many different dimensions and galaxies when I want to be. I have abilities of telepathy and extraordinary awareness when I need them. I feel my inherent connection and oneness with everything that exists in the universe.

I am simply present and curious about everything around me and within me. I feel completely content with what is. I experience a clear field of love around me wherever I go and feel pulled to explore the world and meet with people I'm drawn to within this field. I have a feeling of creativity I want to express in working with others and have absolute confidence the people I'm with will feel this same way.

This state of being that I'm now experiencing more and more is similar to what I experienced twenty years ago after my transcendent awakening; but it's different too, in that there is a groundedness to this new state of being. I feel fully embodied in it. I have brought my body and mind with me into an expanded and clear state of consciousness. I can feel myself both as Consciousness itself—and as form—simultaneously. It is exhilarating.

Floating in the Sea of Love

A number of times over the past couple of years I have experienced another kind of fifth-dimensional experience. It often seems to happen out of the blue. There is generally nothing happening in my life to account for it when it occurs—no event, situation, or relationship that would invoke or create it.

It's this: I'm suddenly aware of feeling as if I'm somehow in a virtual sea of love. There's a soft and pillowy energy all around me, wafting and undulating gently through and around me like waves. I feel held in this watery field of love, tenderly caressed, totally protected.

During these times, every movement I make, every thought I have, is filled with this love—love for myself, love for anyone I think of, love for all of humanity, love for everything that exists. There's the realization that everything *is* love—it's all that exists. We are all simply love expressing in physical form. And I am love, in love with love.

This sea of love, which sometimes sparkles with dancing light, invites surrender—a total giving of myself to it. There is no demand, no push to do this. Yet I willingly fall into it, ready to drown in it if this is what is needed to fully experience its embrace.

I walk through my days when this is happening, almost in a daze or a dream—but I'm actually very present, in the moment. I experience a bright clarity with everything I encounter, whether it's inside of me or outside in my world. There's an easy flow, a sense of well-being that envelopes me, and a radiance that lights my every experience. There's nothing to do but simply be with this radiance.

There are other times when this love seems to emerge from deep within me—like a gush of water suddenly welling up and completely filling my chest and my whole being, and then spilling out all around me. Often tears of joy accompany these bursts of love that can take me by surprise and come close to overwhelming me.

With some of these experiences, there can sometimes be a simple event I witness that seems to call these love events forth:

something I witness, a few words I hear spoken, or perhaps a look I see in someone's eyes. In the past, although I might have been touched by such things, I know I would not have been so entirely taken over by the feeling of love that reduces me to delicious, blissful mush. It's both the quality and the intensity of these experiences that stun me.

Tsunami of Love

I know deep within that this sea of love that appears both within and around me in all its various forms is the high fourth and fifth-dimensional energy now flowing onto the planet. I believe this love is present here now, fully available to us if we attune to it, open to it, and let it have us.

Others I know are also reporting that they're experiencing it in one way or another. Some have referred to it as the "Tsunami of Love" being sent by the Divine Mother. And this seems to me as good a description of it as any.

My sense is that it exists at a certain vibration, and if we can come into the present moment and shift our awareness to that vibration, we will find ourselves experiencing it. Although, at times, it seems to just find us wherever we happen to be in consciousness. Whether we feel ready for it or not, I believe it's finding its way into our Hearts and taking residence there.

In my experience, this love, very much like water, begins loosening up age-old stuff within my Heart, such as fear, anger, resentment, anguish—emotions that have prevented me, perhaps for lifetimes, from fully experiencing love. It's odd when I experience this "love bath", because I can be totally immersed in the love; and at the same time, I can sometimes also be experiencing an intensely painful emotion that's arising.

I've found it's important, when this happens, to not give full attention to the painful emotion. I can simply note its presence, realize it's been part of my third-dimensional identity—and it recognizes that it's time for it to leave. There is no longer a place for it in my emerging fifth-dimensional consciousness. It's coming up in order to be washed out so even more love may flow in.

One way I've found to understand it is to visualize an old bucket that has residue of old toxic substances that have been stuck to its bottom and sides for years—and now clear, warm water is streaming into it. As the water continues to pour in, the residue eventually softens, comes loose and then begins rising to the top. The toxic substance eventually just spills over the top; and, if I don't grab onto it, it simply washes away and is gone. As time goes on, the bucket gets cleaner and cleaner.

How to Get There

As always, the question that comes up for me any time I reflect on experiences of a higher consciousness like these is: "How can I get into that state of being at will, rather than having to wait for it to appear on its own?"

I used to tell myself that I couldn't bring it on by will—that these experiences were gifts given to me and that I needed to be patient and just wait for them to appear. There is a lot of truth in this—at least there has been in the past. But I'm now realizing that there are some things I can do that can help to guide my awareness into those higher levels of consciousness.

One element that's central is intention. Another is attention. When I just think about wanting to experience that clearer, more joyful state of being, something starts to shift. When I then put my full attention on it, something shifts further. I drop into a deeper awareness. I begin realizing I'm becoming immersed in the present moment, and all thoughts of the future or past are disappearing.

For some, all this may be easier to do with eyes closed. For me, for some reason, it's more effective when I keep my eyes open. As I look out at the world with "soft eyes", everything I see begins changing. There's a deeper aliveness that appears everywhere. And then I'm feeling the aliveness within myself, as well—and soon there's little distinction between what I'm looking at and myself. The borders of separation are disappearing. With this, a quiet bliss begins emerging within me.

And before I know it, I am experiencing what feels like a dimensional shift. I'm floating in new territory, and yet still very grounded. My mind feels empty and clear. There's no need to decide to go anywhere or do anything—everything seems to be happening on its own.

It is not always this easy for me to make the shift into higher consciousness. At times if I'm feeling especially triggered by something, I use "tools" I've learned to assist me, such as the ones I've described at the end of Chapter 4.

I believe we are all finding our own unique ways to shift into fifth-dimensional consciousness. Perhaps this is because we are now in a time when these experiences are simply more available to us than they've been in the past. And perhaps, with both intention and attention, we can guide ourselves into that consciousness in which a part of us is already living.

The more we begin living from that higher consciousness within us, the more we can find it's become our natural, everyday consciousness.

Chapter 13

The Disappearing Self

As wonderful as our 5D experiences may be, it can nonetheless be hard at times to integrate them into our lives. Most of the time, we're kind of half-way in-between our fading third and fourth-dimensional consciousness and our new developing fifth-dimensional consciousness.

Indeed, it can be really strange at times to be part-way through the Ascension process, as most of us are. It becomes clear that aspects of our personality selves are definitely falling away. New aspects are emerging, but we may not relate to them yet. And they don't initially fit comfortably with the other parts that are in the process of disappearing.

And if circumstances in our lives are shifting dramatically, as well, it can all be very disorienting. We can feel somewhat fractured and unintegrated at times.

The only way to make sense of these experiences is understanding that part of us is living in fourth-dimensional reality, with some lingering third-dimensional habit patterns—and part of us is now living in fifth-dimensional reality.

I have a client who says she feels like two different people. When experiencing one self, she feels radiantly joyful and optimistic about life. When experiencing the other, she feels bored to tears about her life, with no interest or passion in anything. "What is going on?" she asks.

Another client tells me she feels she's going crazy. On the one hand, her body is mysteriously feeling more and more pain daily and doctors can't figure out why. She's anxious and depressed about this. Yet she reports she is also simultaneously more awake and happy to be alive than ever before.

I'm sure mainstream mental health professionals would come up with third-dimensional diagnoses for these clients—although they'd likely be puzzled, as both these clients are very clear and lucid and are highly functional. But understanding what I do about the transformation of consciousness now occurring for many of us, I recognize these experiences as signs of Ascension.

I have found a number of ways in which I, too, personally experience this strange transition from one dimension to another.

"Not All Here"

The first is feeling the sensation that I'm "not all here". All of me simply isn't present. And no matter what I do to try to bring myself fully present, it doesn't happen. I'm only partially conscious. I sense another part of me is somewhere else, but I can't access it. So I can't bring both parts together.

It can get really frustrating at times, operating with only partial awareness of where my "self" is. It can even be somewhat scary— like when I'm driving my car. I'm going through all the motions of driving, and even maybe thinking clearly about where I want the car to go, but I'm not sure about anything I'm doing because the full me isn't present. At those times I just have to move into faith that I'm being protected and will get where I want to go in one piece.

There was one time, however, when I was feeling terrified as I was driving my car. The sensation I suddenly had was that of being a small child who was in charge of making a huge chunk of heavy metal go where it needed to go without banging into all the other huge chunks of metal moving around me on the road. I felt petrified at my apparent lack of knowledge of how to safely do this.

In desperation, I finally heard myself demanding out loud to the Powers that Be: "I need ALL of me back here right now! I can't do this alone!" And suddenly, pop! there the rest of me appeared—the aspect of me that was the mature, conscious adult. And with this reappearance came an apology to me: "Sorry! I was handling something really important. But I'm back again with you."

My first reaction was one of tremendous relief. But then the questions came up: Who *is* this that was gone and has now returned? And who am *I*? I never got any clear answer to this, but the understanding that there are obviously different aspects of my being that can operate separately from each other on different dimensions became very clear.

There have been other times I've had a similar experience, but without feeling like a stranded child. For instance, there was a time after I'd recently moved to a new town when I was driving my car through my new neighborhood. All of me seemed to be present. But then, suddenly, it felt as if some aspect of my consciousness that had been gone for quite some time appeared in the car with me. It was a larger aspect of me that felt much wiser and more aware of higher levels of consciousness. I sensed it with me, looking out the windows of the car and murmuring, "So this is where we've moved now? Hmmm—very interesting."

I became aware at that moment that this life I was living on the Earth in human form was perhaps just a "side project" I had going—that there were many other grander, more exciting things that I was involved with on higher dimensions to which I, in this fourth-dimensional body-mind, was not yet privy.

Like with my clients described above, I know talking about these kinds of experiences might make me sound crazy to the average person, so I obviously don't speak much about them.

But I'm never concerned when I actually have the experiences. They're always very real to me, as if I'm being given an opportunity to slip past the usual 3D and 4D veils that separate us from experiencing alternate realities. With each experience, my understanding of myself as a highly complex, multi-dimensional being grows stronger and clearer.

The Absent Self

Another type of disappearing-self experience I've had more and more lately is one in which it feels as if what I've known to be my "self" is actually absent altogether. There's nothing at all here. I am aware of my body, and my mind and emotions—but there's no substance to any of it. It's more than not being familiar with what's present—it's as if my self has actually disappeared.

This sensation can be an incredible relief—it's as if my individual ego self has disappeared and there's nothing left but Consciousness, awareness, presence. I am nothing at all—and yet also everything that exists—both at the same time. This is a familiar experience for me, ever since the transcendent awakening I had two decades ago, and I welcome it every time it appears.

When I'm experiencing this, I feel a natural sense of bliss that carries me from one moment to the next—and yet a deep inner peace that keeps me grounded in the here and now. Fear is absent, self-judgment and unworthiness have disappeared, and love can flood my whole being in a very natural way. It's as if everything is just happening on its own—and I know it's all perfect.

The Observer Self

Another experience of a shifting identity is similar to the "Absent Self"—except that rather than my identification disappearing into Consciousness, I am aware of myself as a point of awareness *within* Consciousness. I'm outside the body, looking in, but it's as if I'm in a different realm of reality.

I'm there in a neutral, detached mode, following behind or above the 4D physical self. I am aware of what's happening inside it, but not identified with it. I'm simply observing.

As this observer, the 4D body-mind is interesting to me but there's a quality of unrealness to it. I can see it's moving and functioning in activity, and also that thoughts and emotions are energetically shifting around inside it. But it almost feels like an empty, illusory shell, or that it exists on a plane that is slowly evaporating.

There's a bliss with this experience of myself, as well, since there's no identification with the mind and emotions and the unrest that can exist with those elements of consciousness. There's simply a deep relaxation and acceptance of all that seems to be unfolding in the moment.

The Emerging Fifth-Dimensional Self

Yet another way I sometimes experience the disappearance of my sense of self is this: the ego self is gone, but there is a feeling of a new, lighter self-existing within the physical body that has replaced it.

It was somewhat disconcerting when I initially experienced this, as it was new and unfamiliar. I realized that all my references points had shifted and there was no solid ground on which to stand. There was very little I could say to describe what was different—and yet, I knew that I was not who I used to be.

Now that this state of being is more familiar, I simply allow the strangeness and the lack of reference points to be what they are. And I discover a sense of deep ease and well-being present, and that my heart and mind are both open to wider vistas of awareness. In this state I feel a natural optimism, a deep trust of what life has in store, a sense of endless possibilities. There's no feeling of lack or limitations. I'm just present in the here and now, enjoying each new moment as it appears.

These last three experiences—a complete absence of an individual self, the observer self, and the emergence of a new self—are now extremely pleasant. I'm aware that third and fourth-dimensional reference points, emotions, and beliefs have been superseded and that each experience is an aspect of fifth-dimensional consciousness.

The Disappearing Third/Fourth-Dimensional Self

But there are other times in which the absence of a sense of self is very different. I'm not knowing myself as pure Consciousness or as the observer; nor am I experiencing a new, lighter self-floating along in life.

All I know in this state is that the person I've known myself to be seems to be slipping away and that my life feels somewhat empty and flat. There's nothing left of my old life that really draws or interests me. This is also a familiar feeling, as I went through the two years I've described earlier of being in what I call the "Void" in which I was living this experience.

In this state, all that remains is my passion for full Ascension into the Fifth Dimension. And thankfully, for the most part this is enough. I write and teach about this phenomenon and give healings to people who are in the midst of the Ascension process. And this is very satisfying and enjoyable.

But there are times when it feels as if there should be something "more". I'm not sure if I'm just missing my old third-dimensional life and its distractions—or whether I'm anticipating what might still be ahead of me, being fully contented with my life.

When in this state of consciousness, I'm not exactly depressed. In fact, I can even experience lovely feelings of love and joy that waft through me in the midst of the emptiness. There's nothing really to complain about. I just feel neutral about everything—no emotional ups or downs. My life just feels small and contained.

It helps to know that this experience of only feeling identified with my third/fourth-dimensional self is what is disappearing. I do know my fifth-dimensional self is present somewhere, but I can't always access it yet at will.

Among other factors, at times I believe my body's feeling of fatigue holds me back from being able to access a higher state of being. Being so much denser than my consciousness, my body is struggling to catch up with me. So I need to be patient and compassionate when I feel sleepy, sluggish, and not quite able to reach into the heights of awareness I am capable of at other times.

Living with the Disappearing Self

In my experience in speaking with friends and clients, it seems that all five of these ways of living with a disappearing self can happen to us in our process of Ascension. And they can all be somewhat disorienting.

And it can get hard when we feel stuck in the evaporating third/fourth-dimensional self. I've found that, if this happens, it's helpful to remember that this limited self is on its way out, and the feeling of flatness and the uncomfortable changes will eventually disappear.

We need to remember that we're in transition from a level of consciousness we've probably lived in for thousands of years into an unfamiliar and much more expansive level of consciousness. It's going to take some time to make the full transition. And the journey there is probably going to be uncomfortable at times.

As time goes on, I think we're going to find that our fifth-dimensional self is claiming us more and more and we're beginning to operate naturally out of its frequency.

Chapter 14

Choosing To Be an Ascension Light Worker

Stepping fully into the role of an Ascension lightworker is not always an easy task. We begin defining ourselves and clarifying our priorities differently. Our interests and perspectives on life change. In the process, we may find relationships with friends and acquaintances with whom we used to enjoying spending time are falling away. This can be disconcerting, confusing and sad.

In particular, many of us who have been on a spiritual path for a long time and shared that process with friends are discovering during these times of Ascension that we are no longer headed in the same direction as many of them are.

I once assumed that everyone on a conscious spiritual path was here on the planet at this time with the specific mission to assist humanity and the Earth through the Shift into the Fifth Dimension. I have since realized this may not be so. This became apparent to me when I realized that some of my spiritually-focused friends would light up immediately when I'd begin speaking about the Shift occurring on the planet—and some wouldn't at all.

Some of them would be right there with me, excited about the planetary transition into the Fifth Dimension (or at least interested in learning about it). And some people, although very committed to their own awakening and might generally consider themselves "lightworkers", simply didn't relate to it very much.

Not All Lightworkers are Ascension Lightworkers

I think it's useful to understand that those of us who do light up around assisting the Earth and humanity through the Shift into the Fifth Dimension are a particular group of people. We know deep within us that we have volunteered for something very specific this lifetime: we have a commitment to help usher in the new age that we know is dawning for humanity. We are here to assist people through the transition and to help create the New Earth. We have no doubt about this.

We find it strange that certain friends who have been into the same spiritual awakening pursuits with us for years are simply not interested in hearing about Ascension or the New Earth. They can't relate to it. Their eyes kind of glaze over when we start speaking about it. We even sense judgment from them, as if they're thinking we've gone off in a strange and not very enlightened direction.

It's now clear to me that not everyone interested in spiritual awakening has signed up for the same mission that certain other ones of us have. They're undoubtedly here to help contribute to raising the vibration on the planet—but they're not here to focus specifically on it. Their soul purpose or mission may be something else.

That's why when we do find people with the knowing and excitement about Ascension, their friendship can be so precious. And it's why finding community around the Shift, if we can find it, is so valuable.

Completion of the Bodhisattva Vow

Most people I know who are consciously involved in the Ascension process and are moving more deeply into their soul purpose to assist humanity (or at least wanting to begin it) can relate to having taken the Bodhisattva vow at some point in their evolution. This is the vow in the Buddhist tradition to continue incarnating back on the planet over and over again to assist others in their awakening into spiritual freedom—until every last Soul on Earth is free.

This is a serious vow—an incredible commitment requiring a massive amount of compassion for humanity. I've known for a long time that I at one time took that vow (or maybe even numerous times in different lifetimes). And there have been times in this lifetime when I've wondered if I could possibly get out of it.

I always saw the process of every Soul on Earth becoming free as an incredibly long, slow and arduous one, probably stretching over thousands of years. And I have felt such a soul-deep weariness this whole lifetime. How could I continue until the end of time, living through even one more lifetime on Earth?

And then I received inner guidance one day that this is what Ascension is all about. Every Soul on Earth who desires freedom and full awakening (either consciously or unconsciously) now has the opportunity to achieve it. This isn't going to take thousands of years more of reincarnating over and over again—it's going to happen in a relatively short period of time.

We are actually at that beginning point now: it may be only a matter of a few decades, or even less for many of us. And, according to some sources, most people will not even have to leave their current body to experience it—they will shift into the Fifth Dimension with the body they now have.

It feels so good to realize that my involvement in assisting others to realize what is happening in the Ascension process is actually bringing my Bodhisattva vow to completion. Whether other people consciously get what is happening—or feel excited about the fact that it's a planetary-wide phenomenon—is irrelevant.

All that matters is that every Soul left on the Earth when it ascends will be returning to full consciousness. And that brings me unbelievable joy.

Specific Preparations for Ascension Lightworkers

Something else I've noticed: Those of us who know we are specifically Ascension lightworkers are also moving very rapidly and intensely through the clean-out phase involved in the Ascension process. While we're experiencing many incredibly beautiful and exciting awakening breakthroughs, the changes and losses in our lives are also whirling through us, sometimes one after another.

Most people around us are going through their usual lives, with perhaps more stress than ever before, but without any real sense that something new is unfolding. Yet many of us are living lives with unusual and dramatic shifts. "Tests" are showing up regularly to help us let go of old dysfunctional patterns, relationships that no longer work, and identities that no longer fit. Depressions and anxieties show up out of nowhere. There's a feeling of being thrust into the Unknown without a roadmap.

Perhaps we are all being prepared to be wayshowers and guides for when things truly begin to fall apart on the planet, something predicted to happen for the near future by visionaries and indigenous elders for a long time. (Actually, you don't have to listen to visionaries to get that this is already in the process of happening—you just need to follow the news and connect the dots.)

Whenever our lives start flying apart, it's good to remember who we are and what our purpose is as Ascension lightworkers. We need to keep the bigger picture in mind and know that there's a purpose to all that is occurring in our lives and in our being.

It's also helpful to remember that we're not alone in this process. Not only do we have immense support from the invisible realms, but on this physical realm as well. Ascension lightworkers are waking up all over the world. There will soon be more and more opportunities for us to work together to usher in the emerging new age.

We can relax knowing that we will all find our places with each other—and fulfill what we've come here to do.

And yet, and yet...what about all those friends we used to relate to so well who are not in this group? What I've found is that if there is still a heart connection between us, and as they continue on their own path of awakening, no matter how different from mine at this point, I can continue to enjoy being with them.

At the same time, if our friends don't continue on with a commitment to their spiritual paths, our friendship with them may fade. We will have increasingly fewer reference points in common.

Valuing our Current Friends

As this shift has happened in my own life, I find that I look toward those friends who are focused on their Ascension process and find I am valuing them more than ever. I am sometimes overwhelmed with my love for them and with gratitude that they are in my life. I feel profoundly how precious they are to me.

If we happen to have a misunderstanding, I seem to have greater and greater ability to quickly move out of my own point of view and into a deeper understanding and tolerance of the other person's experience. Love arises in me more quickly. I experience greater ease in owning my own stuff and being transparent and honest about my feelings. And I notice these same things happening with the other person. There's more spaciousness between us, less reactivity.

I'm hearing similar reports from others around me. I perceive these as signs of the shift we've made into the higher Fourth Dimension. The energies in this dimension are calmer, more spacious, giving us room to choose our responses to each other, rather than reacting out of habit. We have the opportunity to move into our hearts more easily and respond with compassion and understanding.

Chapter 15

Shifting Identity

One of the questions many of us may be asking at this point, after all the challenges and shifts we've experienced throughout our Ascension process thus far is: What actually has changed for us? Is there anything tangible we can point to that feels different from what might have happened anyway if Ascension weren't occurring?

I have found myself asking this very question. Am I actually changed in any significant way? Has my life become different, hopefully better and more satisfying? What exactly am I experiencing?

I've come up with some surprising answers to these questions that are very encouraging. In fact, I've realized there are times these days when I actually marvel at how different I am. It's as if I hardly know myself anymore.

Are the Shifts Permanent?

I need to note at this point that there's a habitual third-dimensional part of me that shudders to think I am putting these changes I believe have happened for me down in black and white in a book. It wonders: *What if these shifts aren't permanent? What if I lose these new realizations and it ends up that nothing has really changed? I'll feel like a fool.*

I have to admit that these fears could come true. But I am taking a chance in recording the changes anyway. All of the shifts I describe below have been fairly stable for quite a while now. And even if I do end up "losing" them at some point, I figure I will still have experienced them, and I therefore know they are possible for me. I can experience them again.

But more importantly, I keep getting the inner message that the shifts all of us are experiencing are permanent; we are not going to be falling back anymore, once we begin moving through the

Ascension experience. If we do seem to return to old patterns, relationships and situations, it's not an actual return: it's a revisit to a point further up on a spiral.

In other words, we revisit the experience from a higher level of consciousness. It's like a review of what we've left behind from a new perspective and with more understanding. And it's easier to simply move on without getting caught in the same emotions and thoughts as before.

My hope in describing all the shifts I've been experiencing is that they may be similar to ones that may be happening for you, as well. Or they may spark an awareness of other shifts you have made. It's important to validate these shifts to give ourselves encouragement to continue on in our Ascension process.

Shift in Mood

One of the major things I can name at this point is subtle but absolutely huge: I am experiencing an on-going feeling of "human happiness". I distinguish this from "spiritual joy", an emotion I have often had, especially in the last twenty years or so. Spiritual joy happens when I am filled with elation and an utter knowing of who I am. It's an amazing state of being and I'm always deeply grateful when I can experience it.

But human happiness is something that until recently has eluded me most of my life. This experience, in my vocabulary, is simple contentment about myself and my life—a happiness engendered by the "usual" things in which other people claim to find contentment.

Some people seem to inherit this quality and have it from birth. Due perhaps to a genetic abundance of serotonin—or just plain "good karma"; they seem to be naturally happy most of the time, almost no matter what's happening. Others seem to garner a sense of happiness from certain important events in their life and from their relationships.

But others of us do not seem to have happiness as an inherent quality, nor can we sustain it for any length of time when pleasurable circumstances arise. Since childhood and especially since the onset of puberty, I can remember only a default mood I lived in that I would call melancholy, even depression at times.

Of course there were difficult events and situations in my childhood which would seem to account for this mood. But even when I moved into adulthood and began experiencing circumstances in my life that probably would have brought happiness to someone else, I could never quite feel that sense of simple happiness about myself or my life—or at least sustain it when it might show up for a short while. Unless something particularly great was currently happening at the moment, my mood would just naturally move toward melancholy.

I learned through hard work over the years how to create a mood of happiness and relate to others from that place, and many would be surprised to hear me say I was a naturally depressed person. But people who know me well would concur with what I am saying. I indeed lived through many periods of my life fighting depression and suicidal ideation. I would have, at any point, given almost anything to leave the planet if I could have done so without a lot of fuss and without leaving loved ones behind in pain.

So it is with great surprise and delight that I can now say that this default mood of depression is no longer with me. As I've described earlier, there are times when a dullness or flatness still find their way into my experience. But even in these times, there is an awareness of what is actually true and real, so the old depression does not claim me. In fact, that old familiar state of mind feels part of an obsolete identity that is no longer available to me as a choice. It's as if I've left it behind me somewhere along the way, discarded.

There's no outer event, change in circumstance, or relationship I can point to, to account for this change. It has simply crept into being without my necessarily noticing it. What I find almost shocking is when I check into the area of my lower three chakras, I find a stunning near-absence of fear—something that has, until lately, always been there. Instead I find self-confidence, an optimism about abundance, and a deep feeling of well-being.

This is nothing short of miraculous. If nothing else at all were to happen in my Ascension process, just this would be worth every challenge and loss I've gone through in the last number of years.

I am finally content to be in this aging human body, living my rather unexciting life, even without the many things I always thought I needed to have in order to be happy. I feel happy for no particular reason. And I am naturally optimistic, even when a situation doesn't seem to merit it. I just expect everything will always turn out well in the end. I have a deep trust in the divine orchestration that seems to occur constantly in my life.

I am blessed with truly knowing that happiness is something that happens from within, no matter what might be happening in my life or to my body. And I don't have to work for it—it's a natural state of being with which I am now blessed.

I believe this natural state of happiness is our birthright—that if it's not already happening, it will be at some point for all of us. Beliefs and emotions that have kept us in fear, anger and grief are dropping away and are harder to sustain when they do arise. It is all part of the natural path toward fifth-dimensional consciousness.

Shift in Self-Confidence

Another important shift in my personality structure is a marked increase in my sense of self-confidence. Without any effort these days, even when something is occurring that would have previously made me feel inadequate or self-conscious, I move quite naturally into a feeling of self-confidence, a lack of self-doubt.

This has not always been so for me. For most of my life, I suffered from feeling self-conscious about myself. I also had much difficulty in accepting compliments or hearing people tell me I must feel really good about my accomplishments. I could never quite relate to myself as being "successful", no matter what I had created or accomplished, even when others would enumerate all that I had succeeded in doing on my own.

Greater Sense of Success and Inner Power

Now I'm constantly surprising myself. I not only feel successful and self-confident, I actually feel that I have a commanding presence at times, emanating a great deal of inner power. It feels natural and comfortable. And it isn't based on anything in particular I've done or am involved with.

I may have always had this sense of power about my presence (and can even remember people telling me about it and not being able to relate to it); but the difference is now I am feeling it myself and accepting it as part of who I am. My self-worth and identity are not so attached to what I do anymore or how I might feel I am succeeding. They're just a part of who I *am*.

Greater Detachment and Inner Strength

Along with this comes a greater sense of detachment about how I look or present myself to people. To some extent, I think this is something that just comes with age—there's less caring about what other people think about me. But I was greatly challenged in this area last year, when I started going out to speak about the book I'd just published.

Just one week before I was to speak at my first engagement, a startling thing happened: As I was eating dinner one evening, one of my front top teeth fell out, totally unexpectedly. It just broke off. And I was left with a huge gap in my mouth—one week before I was to give my first presentation.

It was really horrifying to suddenly be without a large tooth at the front of my mouth; I couldn't even look at myself in the mirror for the first few weeks without cringing. It was as if I'd lost a hand or some other part of my body.

I was able to see the dentist the next day; and within the week, I had an appliance in my mouth with a false tooth attached to it— which was the good news. The bad news was that this appliance (known as a "stayplate") was extremely uncomfortable, and speaking clearly with it was very challenging. When I was wearing it, I could never quite forget about it, as it was a large and hard encumbrance in my mouth.

It was stressful, to say the least, to make my debut presentation just one day after I'd gotten the stayplate—and I was anxious. Yet, thinking back on this—and on the other presentations and interviews I gave while wearing this appliance—it's amazing to me how much I took it all in stride. Speaking clearly was not easy, and my mouth constantly got dry. And yet I just went ahead and did what I needed to do.

This type of detachment and inner strength wasn't totally foreign to me; I've always been a person who could just "soldier on", even after disasters have happened in my life. But there was a difference in this experience: It felt relatively easy and smooth. I didn't feel as if I was pushing myself or hiding painful emotions as I might have in the past.

There was a new ease I was feeling about life, an ease in my every day activities, and an ease in meeting unusual challenges. This experience of ease seems to be one of the hallmarks of living in a higher vibration. Less stress, less hurry, less anxiety.

Disappearing Monkey Mind

Another remarkable shift I'm noticing is the immensely quieter mind I'm living with these days. The noisy, irritating, constantly-busy monkey mind that used to drive me crazy is all but absent.

Quiet Mind

For the most part, there's a deep quiet reigning in my head. Not much going on at all. I call this state of mind "quiet mind". When thoughts do arise, it's as if they arise out of nowhere—and then disappear back into nowhere, unless I follow them into other thoughts. But even this process has a slow and quiet rhythm to it now.

When I'm engaged in conversation with another person, more thoughts are naturally activated and emotions can also arise. But the thoughts and emotions all seem relevant and consistent in the moment with what I'm saying or hearing from the other person. My mind doesn't feel over-active or anxious to express more thoughts.

Empty Mind

Then there's a deeper state of mind I more and more often experience that I identify as "empty mind". This is a consciousness that often happens within meditation and for a while afterwards. There are no thoughts at all present in this state, no activity or movement happening within my mind.

I'm simply aware of the spaciousness that I essentially am, and the subtle bliss that exists within this spaciousness. And I'm also conscious of a feeling of profound relaxation I'm experiencing in my body. It's delicious. When thoughts do begin to appear again, they start out at the "back" of my mind—very quiet, subtle and faint.

No Mind

More recently, I've become aware of yet a deeper state of being in which I am conscious that the mind is simply absent altogether. It's not just quiet or empty: it's just not present at all.

Until my first experience of this, I had not been fully aware of how the mind is like a filter that exists between me and the outer world. Everything I perceive, I perceive through this filter. When my mind is busy or my emotions are activated, what I am perceiving outside myself is always affected by—and often distorted by—my beliefs, thoughts, emotions and prior experiences.

Over time, with much personal work, these distortions have grown paler and less powerful, and I'm able to perceive the world more accurately. But even as refined a filter as my mind has become, it's still a filter. It's something through which I usually experience the world.

With this new experience of "no mind", it's as if even the very refined filter is not present. There's a direct and clear experience of me and the outer world. There's an awareness that there's me and there's something else I'm perceiving and relating to with nothing between us.

Paradoxically, there is also no difference between me and whatever I'm perceiving. Yet I haven't disappeared into Consciousness; I'm still an individualized aspect of it. There's just nothing even faintly separating me from the rest of the world in form.

When I find myself in this state, it's as if I've awakened into a new reality—one that's at once very familiar, yet fresh and alive. It's similar to when I'm watching a movie in black and white, and then suddenly everything turns into color.

All three of these experiences with the mind are incredible blessings. After living so long with such an active mind, it's an amazing relief to walk around in even the "quiet mind" experience most of the time now. With this, life is generally light, smooth and steady.

Energetic Shift in Sense of Self

Some of the most exciting shifts I can note at this point in my sense of identity are energetic. As I feel into myself, I am sensing an increasing feeling of empty, clear space inside. There's more light, more fluidity. I'm not as dense-feeling.

It's as if my molecules are spinning further apart from each other. There are times when I'm almost surprised that I can't walk through walls or that solid objects don't just pass through me.

A Larger Self

I also often experience myself as being a whole lot larger than my physical body. Although I used to believe that we are much more than our bodies and minds and that we have more chakras than the ones we know about in the body, it was all pretty much theory to me. I couldn't actually feel this to be true.

In the last few years, especially after my experience as the "magnificent self" I described in Chapter 10, it has now become a reality and a very tangible aspect of my identity. I can feel myself being much taller and vaster than my physical body, and I am aware of myself at the 8th and 9th chakras above my head and sense the further chakras above.

As time goes on, it's as if lights are suddenly going on in different aspects of my consciousness and in my sensation of who "I" am. Suddenly I am aware of who I am in a whole new place within myself that I have not previously even known existed. I am awake in my pineal center. I am awake in the place somewhere above my head that is contact with universal mind. I am awake in the aspect of my spiritual heart that connects directly to the collective consciousness.

These are actual experiences, somewhat kinesthetic in nature, not simply an intellectual understanding about them. They are places within me that have always been there; they've just been dormant until I woke up to their existence and found myself conscious in them.

A Higher Perspective

I am increasingly experiencing an awareness of myself as a being that I can't even quite call "human". I can't say exactly *who*— or what—I actually am during these times, but I find myself at a remove from the human race and I'm observing human beings as if I'm not one of them myself.

In these experiences, as I observe humans, enormous love and compassion suddenly well up inside of me for this race of beings— as well as a kind of awed respect. I marvel at the courage all humanity has demonstrated in making its way through the Third Dimension with so much ignorance and lack of direct contact with the Divine.

And such a profound joy erupts in me, a sense of triumph, in realizing humanity is on its way back to reawakening. It's as if I've been waiting forever for these times of awakening to come, and that I've been rooting for so long with all my heart for humanity to make it through.

This happened one night recently as I was watching a video. It was a tender, heart-felt film about a man and his sixteen-year-old daughter who were meeting for the first time since her birth. As it turned out, they both happened to write and play music. And, predictably, at the end of the film they were playing music and singing together. It was a sweet scene and probably would have brought a few tears to my eyes in the past.

But I suddenly found myself sobbing. Not in a sentimental kind of way—and it wasn't about the actors or the characters they were portraying. It was more that I was seeing them suddenly as representative of human beings on this planet—and realizing how difficult life truly is for such asleep souls who have been stranded so far from home.

And then I was thinking: "But look—humans have created music! This is one thing that has helped get them through this long, dark passage of the Third Dimension. How moving—and how clever they are!" And my heart was just breaking with love and joy for all of humanity.

Merging with the Soul

For most people, I think, the idea of a "Soul" is likely just a concept. Many imagine it as something invisible that exists somewhere inside of them, perhaps as an energy they feel in their heart or a knowing of a higher experience of themselves. There's a shift of awareness or a deepening that occurs when they focus on it. But there isn't a fully conscious experience of knowing the Soul.

At some point, I think many of us may have moved past a mental conception of the Soul into a deeper knowing of it. I made this shift myself; and in fact, I could have said that I knew what the experience of actually knowing the Soul was.

But I now know that the feeling back then still had an imaginative or mental quality to it. Today I am knowing the Soul in a much more tangible, experiential way. It's very clear to me that it is a distinct consciousness, a felt presence that has an extremely refined substance to it. When I am fully immersed in it, I become aware of a subtle, powerful sense of a "motor" humming deep inside of me that feels profoundly comforting.

More and more, I feel myself merging with this essence. There's a sensation that it is all around me and that it's in the process of fully entering my physical body—or should I say, that my body is entering more fully into it. And, as time goes on, I realize that often I feel completely surrounded and immersed in its energy. I am merged with it; I know it is who I am.

This experience is somewhat different from the transcendent awakening experience I've described earlier that I had twenty years ago. In that experience, I knew myself as pure Consciousness and that everything "out there" was actually a part of Me—or perhaps more accurately, I was a part of it. There was no more individual me.

This new experience of merging with the Soul has been similar in that I often feel there are no boundaries between me and the outside world; but rather than an absence of self, there is a sense of myself as an individual self that is infinite.

I also feel protected and safe, as well as more empowered. Something new, and yet very familiar, is now with me—a presence that I once knew, but had forgotten. And it is becoming more and more who I am: a Soul using a body and mind to experience physical reality.

Thinking from the Heart

Another interesting phenomenon I experience from time to time is a sense of thoughts actually coming out of the center of my chest—from my heart—rather than from my head. In the past whenever I'd hear that in fifth-dimensional consciousness we will "think with our hearts", I believed this to be a metaphorical expression. I now know that it's actual. Thoughts can come directly from the area of the heart.

The thoughts I experience coming from my heart are of a high vibration. They also seem to carry much more with them than just mental ideas. It's as if there's some sort of coding in them that carries information I'm absorbing on an unconscious level, information from a much higher source than my rational mind.

Developing Psychic Abilities

Although I've been blessed in my life with certain abilities that might be called somewhat "psychic"—such as an ability to sense things about people I haven't been told about, an ability to remember some of my own past lives, and a common knowing of who is calling me on the phone—these have been abilities that never felt very remarkable or finely honed.

But in the past year or so, I can definitely say that all my psychic senses have been opening up and developing very rapidly. Seeing, hearing, feeling—or just simply knowing things past the ordinary ways of knowing—have all become surprisingly clear and seem to continue becoming more available.

These abilities are quite delightful to have, and they are very helpful in the sessions I now offer to people. Yet I find there are responsibilities that go along with them. I need to be discerning when I think to share what it is I am seeing about a person. And I need to keep clear of any ego tendencies of wanting to demonstrate or talk about the abilities, unless it happens to be appropriate.

This development of psychic abilities is something else that seems to be happening for others I know, as well. The veils are getting thinner. And from what I understand, these abilities we call "psychic" are abilities we all inherently had before the Fall of Consciousness—so it makes sense that as we move closer to the Fifth Dimension, we will be rediscovering them.

Indeed, I believe almost anyone these days can probably develop psychic abilities with a little effort. It's just a matter of tuning into a certain aspect of our consciousness where information, images and messages appear. It demands paying attention to those times our intuition speaks to us and exploring where within our body or being they came from. Then it's a matter of focusing our attention there and identifying that "place" we can go to when we're looking for information.

And then, of course, it requires that we trust that what we're receiving is accurate. This is a process that usually requires some practice. Believing faint images or messages to be real and accurate can initially be scary. The question usually comes up: "But is this real? Is it true? Or is it something my mind has just conjured up?"

Until you're certain these communications are authentic, try trusting them for a short while. And if possible, check them out. Do they jive with other information you have available? Do they resonate with the person you're hearing something about? The more you do this, if you have a sincere desire to be in integrity and to cause no harm to anyone, you'll find that your images, messages and knowing will become increasingly clear, and you'll begin trusting yourself more and more.

Shifts in Everyday Life

All of these experiences and changes in my personality and my sense of identity are fantastic, and it's helpful for me to name them. It makes all the inner work I've done to move along my Ascension path worthwhile.

However, until about a year ago, I wouldn't have said that those inner shifts, as wonderful as they were, had made any difference in my life's manifestations. I was still living a very small, contained life in which I was feeling little passion. I certainly wasn't discovering what my soul mission was—or if I even had one.

New Work

Then it seemed to happen all at once—the thrust into a new life. It started with the writing of my last book. This seemed to occur out of nowhere, after living in my "incubation cave" for two years and doing nothing that was at all satisfying in the world of work.

I had given up a full-time practice of spiritual counseling when I'd gotten sick 15 years before; and aside from a two year period in which I was giving *deeksha* and holding classes and individual sessions a few years ago, I had ceased doing anything that resembled what my career had always been—assisting people on their spiritual path.

I was fortunate enough to have a minimally-satisfying job of internet writing that sustained me financially through some of those years, and I was grateful for this. And, because all motivation to go back to my former work was gone, I imagined I would probably live out my life doing similar mind-numbing work. I was finally surrendered to this and lived with a sense of peace believing I had apparently "completed" my real work in the world.

Little did I know how untrue this was. After writing this last book (and coming totally alive in the process), I suddenly found myself out in the world, speaking about the Fifth Dimension. I was also giving internet radio interviews on the subject—and totally enjoying this. I was amazed at how it all came about so quickly.

Then within a matter of months, I suddenly found people asking for Quantum Healing sessions that I had previously been giving only to myself. I soon found I was adding my own particular twist to the healings: receiving messages from people's guides and information about past lives that related to the healings.

This work quickly became extremely satisfying to me, filling me with a feeling of being right on the mark in doing what I'm here to do at this point. Before I knew it, giving these healings mushroomed into a full-time practice.

Financial Abundance

And, miracle of miracles, it also meant that for the first time in my life, I was truly experiencing an ease around creating financial abundance. I still marvel at this transformation.

I feel so grateful about the shifts that have happened in this last year in my life, that I am at times overcome with gratitude and have to stop whatever I am doing to just take in the miracle. There are even times when I suddenly stop and look at myself, wondering, "Who is this woman who is living this life now?" She feels like someone I don't quite know yet. It's very strange.

Increased Synchronicities and Manifestation

Something else I've noticed in my life and hear from others as well is that synchronicities seem to be increasing in our lives. Manifestation is also happening much more quickly. We barely think of something we might want or need, and the next day it's there for us. It can feel like magic; but in the Fourth Dimension, manifestation does happen more quickly than in the Third Dimension.

This is good news if we're thinking positive thoughts and we're focusing on what we want and need, rather than on what we don't. But even if we aren't, when we manifest something quickly, it's much easier to see that we are indeed manifesting our own reality.

Speeding up Our Ascension Process

Can we speed up our Ascension process? I believe we can. I know I am fortunate in having all these shifts into higher consciousness happening as quickly as they are. But I assume this is because I've chosen two methods of inner work in the last five years that I believe have accelerated my progress a great deal: An intensive program in learning Quantum Healing with Dell Morris for three years, and then being part of the Mastering Alchemy program that Jim Self offers for the last two years.

Both of these programs involve intense inner work and dedication—and a lot of motivation to work through whatever is arising in one's personal Ascension process. And I definitely have had this motivation to clear out my third-dimensional baggage. I came in with a lot of it this lifetime, and have throughout my adulthood done one thing or another to heal childhood traumas, as well as those from other lifetimes.

There are many programs available these days similar to the ones I've chosen that can assist people to move more quickly and smoothly through the Ascension process—to both empty out old limiting patterns and emotions and to open up to the new energies that are now available on the planet.

But it's clear that speed is not necessary. I know I am generally impatient when I can see and feel something I really want to experience, and I tend to jump in with both feet when I decide to do something. But I know this isn't the only way to go about it. We each have our own natural way.

I believe that even if we don't choose to move quickly—or even to move through Ascension in a conscious way—it is still happening. Perhaps a little more slowly. Perhaps a little rockier and with shifts that are more dramatic. Or maybe it's actually smoother and easier, since it's slower. There's no knowing, as we are all unique.

But one way or another, those of us who have chosen to shift into the Fifth Dimension are all moving through the changes we need to make at the speed we've chosen to make them—and there's no right or wrong way to do this.

Soul Missions

In addition, I'd say that in my experience, not all of us are moving into our Soul missions in the way I have, in such an accelerated manner. Many are discovering their purpose as an Ascension lightworker more gradually through shifting from one career to another, or shifting within the work they're already doing so that they're doing it in a clearer way, with fewer ego agendas attached.

And there are those who are still waiting for their missions to begin. I have clients who feel passionate about what they know their soul mission to be and are entirely ready to enter into it. But nothing yet is on the horizon. Now that it has happened for me after believing it would probably never even happen at all, I can say with a lot of certainty that if someone feels they have a mission they've signed up for, then they do have one. It simply may not yet be quite right timing for it to unfold.

I do believe, however, the time is coming when all those who have signed up to be Lightworkers during this time of Ascension will be discovering their missions soon. The world is changing rapidly, and there is plenty of light work to be done. So I don't think it will be long before we're all on track, working together to help bring about the shift of the Earth and humanity to the Fifth Dimension.

Chapter 16

Ascension Is Happening

It's clear that Ascension is a complex and paradoxical process—one involving both joy and grief, confusion and clarity, and power and vulnerability. It's also a process filled with surprises, contradictions, and enormous change.

At times it's easier than ever to shift into higher consciousness and experience greater inner freedom, love and peace than we've ever known. And at times it is easier to feel more overwhelmed and helpless than ever. It's an adventure requiring strength, trust, an open heart and a willingness to leap into the Unknown.

We're in the process of incubation—caterpillars transforming into butterflies. And just as cutting open a caterpillar's cocoon reveals a type of mush inside, we can experience ourselves to be that mush—no longer caterpillar, but not yet butterfly either. We're still transforming into what can be considered to be a whole new species of human being.

There's No Avoiding Ascension

There is no avoiding the process of Ascension if we remain here on Earth during these times. It is simply happening. No one can avoid the energies that are emanating from the cosmic field the Earth is now traveling through, which are transforming everything vibrationally into a higher, more awakened conscious-ness.

In this way, as intensely personal as the Shift can be experienced in each of us, it is also an impersonal phenomenon. It's happening everywhere and we are all involved. It's happening whether we feel ready for it or not.

It's much like getting into a car on a rollercoaster. Once we get in, we're committed to wherever the roller coaster is going to take us. We may have some idea of what the experience is going to be like, but we won't know for sure what will happen until it starts moving.

And once we're in the roller coaster, there's no getting off till the ride is over. Our only choice is how we're going to experience the ride. We can take it in fear and clutching and shouting in vain that we want to get off—or we can meet the new and sometimes daunting experiences with courage, determination and a sense of humor. Or a little of all these.

No matter how we take the ride, there's one thing we can rely on if we're committed to it: we will make it through, landing in a whole new consciousness at its end—an entirely new dimension of reality. We will leave all fear, separation and sense of unworthiness behind—along with all other painful and limiting emotions and beliefs.

The Game Is Over

The third-dimensional game is over. It's time to go Home. It's time for us to drop all equipment we've used for playing the 3D game onto the playing field—all hatred, competition, judgment, despair and helplessness. And turn with conscious awareness to return Home together.

We may not know how long this journey will take us, or what we'll encounter along the way. But if we remember that where we're headed is the place we've yearned to return to for eons of time, it will make our journey an easier and more joyful one.

It's important to remember, too, that we're not traveling alone. We can find others traveling in the same direction with the same purpose with whom we can walk. And there are those in the invisible realms also traveling with us, guiding us safely on our way.

Choosing To Be Wayshowers, Guides and Scouts

As we choose to consciously make this journey—and to fully embrace the transformation occurring within us—we can also know we are paving the way for others behind us who are just now beginning to wake up to the fact that the old game is over. We can be wayshowers, guides, and scouts for these people. We can be among those who venture forth ahead of the crowds to see what's up ahead—and then turn around to report what we've seen and experienced.

Such fascinating adventures await us on this rapid journey into the Fifth Dimension! We already have a taste of this awesome exploration in Consciousness and can feel the thrill of meeting these adventures. With great joy and optimism, let us move into whatever is ahead of us with full commitment and trust.

Appendix

What Are Dimensions?

Note: The following information is based on the teachings of Jim Self, Dell Morris and various other teachers and visionaries on the subject of Dimensions within the context of Ascension. All of it resonates with the inner guidance I receive and with my own personal experience.

It's important, first of all, to understand that dimensions are not locations; we are not going anywhere. Dimensions are levels of consciousness that vibrate at certain rates. One way to describe them is as "operating systems" like those in a computer—structures of reality that allow for certain actions, experiences, perceptions and relationships to take place in specific ways.

In order to ascend to a higher dimension, we need to vibrate in resonance with it. Shifting from one level of consciousness to the next higher one means becoming established in the frequency of that consciousness, so we don't unwillingly get drawn back. During the process of Ascension, however, there are times when we can find ourselves shifting back and forth between dimensions, as we "visit" higher dimensions we will eventually be ascending into.

As we shift into higher dimensions, our perception and experience of reality shift because our consciousness has shifted. People, places, and things around us have a frequency that matches the new dimension we've entered. The higher the dimension we exist in, the freer we are to act and create, and therefore greater evolutionary development and spiritual wisdom are required as we shift into higher dimensions.

There exist numerous dimensions: the fourth and fifth are simply higher than the one we've been living in for thousands of years. Within each dimension, there are many levels through which we gradually ascend.

The Third Dimension

The term "third dimension" can be confusing. It might sound as if this refers to the things we see: the chair, the tree, the Earth. In this dimensional context, these things are seen as part of *form*—that which has shape, mass, texture and weight. Form is also present in the Fourth Dimension and to some degree in the Fifth. But in these higher dimensions, things are more light-filled, not as dense as they are in the Third.

Since most of us have lived in the Third Dimension for millennia, it is all we've known as incarnated beings and we therefore assume that how things have operated in this dimensional structure is the only way reality works. But the truth is the Third Dimension, a structure that contains highly rigid and inflexible aspects, structures and limitations, is only one reality structure that exists.

The Rational Mind

While living in this dimension we have evolved to rely on the rational mind to guide us through life, believing it to be the highest, most intelligent system we have available to us. In the higher dimensions, the rational mind is used in a very limited way, seen only as a tool to guide us in relating to physical form. It is not considered the best instrument for helping us to navigate effectively through life. The Spiritual Heart is recognized as the wiser and more powerful guide.

Duality

In third-dimensional consciousness we have a solid belief in duality—up/down, big/small, etc. And often a belief that such opposites as *good* and *bad*, *right* and *wrong*, *should* and *shouldn't* all exist as absolutes. And because of this, judgment, blame, guilt, doubt and fear have been part of everyday existence.

3D Time

While living in the Third Dimension we have also had the perception that time is fixed and linear, and it only moves in one direction—past, present and future. There is no way to move back into the past or to change it. There's no way to be present now in the future. We have assumed that this is the only way to experience time. In higher dimensions, there are different, more fluid, ways to experience time.

Most people have no idea we have shifted out of the Third Dimension or that a great deal more freedom is now available to them to create the lives they wish to live. It will take a while before people give up operating from old habits they formed over thousands of years of living in the Third Dimension, believing in all the programmed restrictions and limitations of this lower dimension.

The Fourth Dimension

As we become aware of the limiting constructs of the Third Dimension, we can begin to step out of our belief that we're still existing in it and move beyond its limits into the much freer atmosphere of the Fourth Dimension. This dimension has been available to us for a number of years; but it's not been until recently when the planet shifted into this dimension in 2012 that it's become totally and easily accessible to us.

Awakening, Well-Being, and Empowerment

Many of us are having more and more experiences of the Fourth Dimension, perhaps without realizing it. The most obvious sign that can indicate we're experiencing this new dimension is when we have experiences of spiritual awakening and heart opening in which we can more easily experience deep inner peace, love and gratitude than before.

We can also be aware of it when we're feeling a sense of clarity, well-being and ease. We feel lighter, less rigid. There's an experience of spaciousness and upliftment, a greater freedom and feeling of empowerment. Everything feels more fluid, less static and fixed; and there's a knowing of endless possibility and a greater opportunity to change what is not working.

The "rules" of the higher Fourth Dimension provide a greater sense of ease and capability. We have an ability to access more power to create what we need and want. We also have a more comprehensive view of reality which brings in a calmer, quieter sense of being. We feel more detached, less reactive to life around us. We can often have a sense of being filled with light.

This is because, in the Fourth Dimension, we have greater access to the essence, power and wisdom of our Soul. As we begin to experience the frequencies of this higher presence flowing into our consciousness, we open to the higher aspects of ourselves and to abilities that allow us to understand reality on a deeper level.

4D Time

Part of the fourth-dimensional experience includes a changing relationship with time. It feels to many of us that time is increasingly passing more quickly, that there is actually less time in a day to accomplish things. However, this experience springs from the fact we are still relating to time from a third-dimensional consciousness.

When we shift into fourth-dimensional consciousness, our experience of time can be very different. In fact, we can feel as if time is actually stretching. We are able to accomplish amazing amounts during a day. This is because time is collapsing in this new dimension into the present moment, into the Now. It is no longer linear.

In the Third Dimension, there was much focus on reacting to the past, and worrying or planning for the future. As we move more and more deeply into the Fourth Dimension, we will be experiencing ourselves more and more in the present moment and not be so concerned about the past and future, except as reference points.

Quicker Manifestation

With this shifting sense of time, we can also become aware that manifestation is much faster than it was in the Third Dimension. We begin to see that if we don't monitor our thoughts, we will very quickly create things we don't want. We have the opportunity to see quite clearly a concept we may have thought we understood before but are now experiencing first-hand: that we create our own reality by the thoughts we think and the emotions we feel.

Choice

In the Fourth Dimension, we can become aware that time is a point of power, in that each new moment is an opportunity for new beginnings and choices we can make.

We now have true choice in how to respond to life—something that did not exist in the Third Dimension. We can choose to change habitual reactions and restrictions we've put on ourselves. We can choose to observe and make choices with clarity and awareness, without judgment or fear of punishment.

We can indeed initiate something new in any given moment. In fact, what is true in one moment can be reversed in the next moment. This can give us an enormous power to change both how we respond to what is happening in our lives—and how it is actually happening. We can experience how our habitual reactive patterns no longer have the hold on us they used to when we were living in third-dimensional consciousness.

For example, if someone has just said something that would normally trigger an angry response in us, we can now see that we have the opportunity to pause for a moment and choose our response. We can move into that habitual reaction—*or* we can choose another response, such as being silent or waiting a few moments and then responding without the anger. By doing this, we have changed the situation, and the direction of our interaction— and even our relationship—with the person can be transformed.

The Fifth Dimension

The Fifth Dimension is a dimension in which all possibilities are available. Even on the lowest levels within this dimension, physical density is much lighter. Form is fluid and the structure of physical bodies has turned to a crystalline form. In this dimension, we will merge and reintegrate with our Soul.

As we progress through the levels of the Fifth Dimension, we will begin to experience who we actually are—truly powerful multi-dimensional beings. Eventually, our full DNA will be activated and the 90% of our brain that's been dormant for thousands of years will come alive again.

As fifth-dimensional beings we will live in ongoing resonance with such feelings as love, joy, enthusiasm, beauty, kindness and reverence. Cooperation, co-creation, and collaboration will come naturally to us as we work and create together.

We will experience psychic abilities we once had long ago, such as telepathy and clairvoyance. Much of what we will experience will pour forth wordlessly from our Hearts, rather than from our minds. Speaking will not be necessary.

As conscious beings, we will progressively be able to access within ourselves information and wisdom that resides in all dimensions. We will experience a oneness with all that is, with no sense of separation. We will think from our Hearts and make Soul-guided choices.

We Can't Take Our Baggage with Us

What's important to understand is that in order to live in the Fifth Dimension where this high vibration exists, all mental and emotional baggage we carry must be left at the door. No fear, anger, hostility, sadness, guilt exists there—no suffering or sense of separation. These emotions and thoughts are all based on the illusion of separation that exists only in the Third and Fourth Dimensions.

In order to be able to achieve this kind of clarity and shift permanently into the Fifth Dimension, most of us need to do a great amount of clearing of negative and limiting emotions, thoughts and patterns that we carry not only from this lifetime, but from many other lifetimes we've lived. It will be a process that will probably stretch over a number of years.

Time in the Fifth Dimension

Time in the Fifth Dimension is even more fluid than in the Fourth. Some describe it as "simultaneous time" or "everything happening at once." We can see all past and future lifetimes simultaneously. We can see all timelines available, all possibilities.

Cycles of day and night still exist, but they're just seen as mechanical markers. They have no effect on the Now that is happening. Perhaps you are already having flashes of this experience of time and haven't been able to put words to it.

Manifestation in the Fifth Dimension is instantaneous: we focus on something in our mind, and it appears. If we look closely, we may see that even now our thoughts are manifesting our future much more quickly. We can practice becoming master of our thoughts—one of the requisites to live in the Fifth Dimension.

Space in the Fifth Dimension

The experience of space in the Fifth Dimension is also quite different from that in the Fourth. In the higher levels, you can simply think of a place, and you find yourself there.

There's also a type of merging that can take place, causing a very different kind of experience when two objects or people come together. For example, in the Third and Fourth Dimensions, if your car hits a tree, both are generally damaged. In the Fifth Dimension, the molecules of the car, you, and the tree simply merge for a bit, then separate again. No damage is done—you've just experienced a moment of unity with both the car and the tree.

When we encounter another being in the Fifth Dimension we can also experience a merging with them when we come together. This is a blissful feeling of actually becoming one unified organism for a while, in which our molecules intermingle with theirs.

When we glimpse these fifth-dimensional experiences, it can be exhilarating. It keeps us moving on through the difficulties that sometimes arise as we travel through the rapid changes in the Fourth Dimension and into the Fifth. And they give us the experience of knowing that Ascension into a higher reality is really happening.

Resources

1. Beckow, Steve: www.goldenageofgaia.com
2. Benedicte, Meg: www.newearthcentral.com
3. Bishop, Karen: *Down into Up*,
   http://ascensioncorner.wordpress.com/
4. Cota-Robles, Patricia: www.eraofpeace.org/
5. Day, Christine: *Pleiadian Principles for Living*,
   http://www.christinedayonline.com/
6. Dillon, Linda: http://counciloflove.com/
7. Hamilton, Craig:
   http://integralenlightenment.com/home.php
8. Hoffman, Brenda:
   http://lifetapestrycreations.wordpress.com/
9. Hoffman, Jennifer: http://enlighteninglife.com
10. Jones, Aurelia Louise: *Telos*, Vols. 1, 2 3
11. Kahn, Matt: http://www.truedivinenature.com/
12. Kenyon, Tom: http://tomkenyon.com/
13. Marx-Hubbard, Barbara: http://barbaramarxhubbard.com/
14. Melkizedek, Drunvalo: *Serpent of Light*,
    http://www.drunvalo.net/
15. Self, Jim: *What Do You Mean the Third Dimension is Going Away?* www.masteringalchemy.com/
16. Ward, Suzi:
    http://www.matthewbooks.com/mattsmessage.htm/

Acknowledgments

With immense gratitude, I wish to acknowledge the extraordinary help Marjorie Bair gave me with her editing comments throughout the writing of this book, as well as her infinite patience as I sought to find the best title for it. I'd also like to thank Shri Estes for her supportive and intuitive feedback on the book at different stages of its completion.

My gratitude extends also to the many people I know who are aware of the Ascension process and have shared with me about their journeys thus far on this path. This includes, very importantly, the dozens of clients I've worked with these last two years who have shared their experiences with me. Some of them may recognize themselves in my stories.

And lastly, I'd like to thank Dell Morris and Jim Self for their teachings about Ascension that validate and support the inner teachings I receive on the subject and continue to support and guide me on my own path.

Vidya Frazier has studied spiritual teachings from both western and eastern traditions for over 40 years. In 1993, she felt called to India to visit the spiritual master Papaji. Upon returning, she wrote *The Art of Letting Go–A Pathway to Inner Freedom* and began offering individual sessions, groups and workshops based on this book.

In 2007, she was invited to attend the Oneness University in India and was initiated as a Oneness Blessing Facilitator. She returned and offered the blessing to hundreds of people. Since then, she has studied with quantum healer Dell Morris and author Jim Self.

In 2014, Vidya published her first book on the theme of Ascension, *Awakening to the Fifth Dimension—A Guide for Navigating the Global Shift* and has given a number of presentations and interviews on the subject.

Currently offering sessions of Ascension counseling and Quantum Healing, Vidya assists people to find their way with clarity and ease through the powerful energies of the Shift of consciousness that is now occurring across the planet. She also assists people in discovering their spiritual purpose in life and stepping more fully into expressing it.

Drawing on thirty-five years as a licensed psychotherapist, hypnotherapist, and spiritual guide, as well as on her own spiritual awakening experiences, Vidya serves as a unique bridge between the worlds of psychology and spiritual awakening.

Contact Vidya at www.vidyafrazier.com.

CPSIA information can be obtained
at www.ICGtesting.com
Printed in the USA
BVHW09s0034090718
521064BV00007B/192/P

9 781506 900605